Literary Constructs of the Self

Literary Constructs of the Self

Socio-Cultural Contexts

Edited by

Santosh Gupta

Mini Nanda

Institute for Research in Interdisciplinary Studies, Jaipur

RAWAT PUBLICATIONS

Jaipur • New Delhi • Bangalore • Hyderabad • Guwahati

ISBN 81-316-0308-3

Published by
Prem Rawat for **Rawat Publications**
Satyam Apts, Sector 3, Jawahar Nagar, Jaipur 302 004 (India)
Phone: 0141 265 1748 / 7006 Fax: 0141 265 1748
E-mail: info@rawatbooks.com
Website: www.rawatbooks.com

New Delhi Office
4858/24, Ansari Road, Daryaganj, New Delhi 110 002
Phone: 011 2326 3290

Also at Bangalore, Hyderabad and Guwahati

Typeset by Rawat Computers, Jaipur
Printed at Chaman Enterprises, New Delhi

Dedicated to

Professor Meenakshi Mukherjee

whose writings reflect the evolution of the creative self in its myriad forms.

Contents

Introduction

To know one's self has been a persistent and perennial human endeavour and has been the foremost concern of disciplines like Philosophy, Psychology, Literature, and Religion. Yet it remains an elusive entity, reinvented constantly across the flow of time, experiences and the process of being.

Human cognitive and imaginative faculties have taken different directions and paths to the realization of the multi-layered and multi-shaded complex reality of the inner core of being, called the self. While Philosophy seeks to understand it in abstract terms, literary writers usually place it within the quotidian and empirical frameworks, and try to work out the evolving self as it relates to the external world. For all the writers who chase this chimera the externalization of the conceptuality of this awareness becomes an engagement of the inner self with the objective correlative that they look for. The writer's own self becomes engaged with the world outside, and is often expressed through new, imagined selves.

Writing about the self becomes, at times, the process of constructing a self as it appears in the text. Kabir used the trope of weaving a fabric as he spoke about God as the Supreme Weaver and the soul as a fabric, a *chadariya*. He wrote about the mystic, divine as well as the social aspects of the selfhood that relates to these dimensions or levels of reality. Walt Whitman, too, spoke about the self as he sang 'One Self I Sing'. In his poems the material aspect predominates the vision of a self forever flowing towards other human beings, of all races, colours and origins.

Singing about the self, or portraying its interaction with the Others, writers see the self as being formed within the given contexts. Constructing the self depends upon perception, conceptualization and a selection from the private experiences; sometimes the writer creates a 'persona' or a mark to attain a level of detachment from the created self/selves. These strategies are crucial and critical in the aesthetics of the self where memory, language and heightened imaginative self-awareness become main components.

The reconstruction of the past, whether at a personal level or of the family, community or nation has an importance place in the writing of the self. Memories, history and legends, coalesce in the life of a public figure like Mahatma Gandhi, whose personal life is enacted on a public stage of the national movement. Constructing fully and finally a self of such a figure eludes writers, even as many attempts are made to portray him. Similarly, in the works of writers like U.R. Ananthamurthy, D.H. Lawrence, Caryl Phillips and Amitav Ghosh, the characters they create do not represent the life of a single individual. Their characters (some of them, especially) incorporate a whole generation's feelings, dreams or conflicts.

For most literary writers creating the self within the page becomes a negotiation between the I and Thou, the self and the other, the individual and the community. As they organize their memories and experiences a careful selection is made which gives shape and form to the indefinable and fluid self. The narrative of self-awareness that is formed bears a clear imprint of a carefully conceived and organized effort at imposing 'a narrative on a life' that, as Edward Said puts it, one had left as 'disorganized, scattered, uncentred' (556). Since actual life is in a constant state of flux, the process of imposing an order becomes useful in giving it a clearly recognizable shape.

Writing about one's own self or about imagined (other) selves can become for the writers an existential exercise of re-constructing one's self; It can also provide some therapeutic relief as one goes over the losses, mistakes and experiences of one's life. It is a process that involves both the writer and the readers, who respond to the persons within the texts as images, icons or reflections of real human beings.

The essays included in this volume explore the process of writing the self from two perspectives: from that of the creative writers as well as the readers on different literary presentations of the self. The essays that look into the creative process share the intimate and extremely elusive forms of awareness and impressions of the writers, as they strive to give shape, form, voice, and body to shadows within their mind. The search for a proper shape and habitat of the imaginary shadows within a perceptive and creative artist engages them with their social, historical and cultural milieu of their age. The primary inspiration comes from a desire to embody the elusive human self into a concrete context and give it a meaning. Literature has been concerned for the most part with the human quest to attain deep and full knowledge of the self, for that knowledge is related to epistemology, moral and ethical philosophy and religion. The quest for knowing the self has inspired human endeavours through diverse methods, modes, leading individuals to different mediums of expression. We have presented here essays from both, the creative writers as well as critical readers. Some of the most respected of Indian writers have penned their views on the self, their own forms of writing and the artifices they use. Their observations on some of the influences they have had also indicate to some extent their own intellectual journeys. The creation of one's own self, or of imagined characters, in one's short and longer fictional writing in a self-analytical manner, lays bare some of the mystique of writing.

Critical readings of fictional and other literary forms where the construction of the self is foregrounded forms the second set of essays in the volume. These essays explore the use of various modes in presenting the self, in all its heterogeneity, multilayered and ambivalent forms. The essays do not search for philosophical dimensions of the quest for self as an abstraction; they rather see the interrelatedness between the individual and the immediate surrounding social and cultural milieu. Most of the contributors in this volume write about the self from an existential and experiential base, for the development of a 'self' is seen as one of the most crucial of one's needs in life. This self however does not become a fully developed, fixed entity, rather it is formed as it is perceived and comprehended.

The focus is on both the process of *Writing the Self* and on the different forms of self-awarenesses: how it is imagined, how the awareness crystallizes and then transformed through devices like myths, metaphors, tropes and narratives. Pure consciousness, the subject-matter of abstract philosophy, has to be seen in material context and form, the way most human beings experience it. This is the view of philosophers like Edmund Husserl and other phenomenologists and existentialists. Husserl maintains that consciousness is always given to itself, and that the word 'consciousness' has no meaning independently of this self-givenness (Merleau Ponty, 488). It is felt by many writers that to be aware of oneself is not to capture a pure self that exists separately from the physical and intellectual contexts in which one is placed, rather, it is to be conscious of one's experience in the implicit first person mode of givenness. They view awareness of the self to be embodied and embedded in the world that has specific temporal, spatial frames of experience. The self, as viewed by most of the contributors is never a viewpoint from nowhere, it is always defined by the situation of the perceiver's body, its location, a particular social position and which performs actions in pragmatic contexts and interactions with other people.

There is also the view that intersubjective actions and field of activity makes social presence play a determining role in the growth of self-awareness. Creative writers, whose essays appear in this volume, seem to believe, as Sartre has put it 'our being, along with its being for itself, is also for others, the being which is revealed to the reflective consciousness is for itself for others' (Sartre, 282). The formation of the self is imperceptibly moulded by geographical and temporal specificities. Edward Soja, an important modern writer, has brought into focus the geographical locations as a formative influence on self-awareness. The nineteenth century thought was predominantly concerned with history and time, but in the twentieth century the impact of large-scale spatial dislocations and displacements, the emergence of exile, diaspora and travelling on a voluntary basis in search of attaining different forms of freedoms, fulfilments and self-expression have made the consideration of space critically important. These dislocations, Soja argues, have influenced deeply the human sense of (un)belonging, (up)rootedness and the yearning for a fixed single home. When a large number of people who have lost their sense of belonging permanently begin to express that feeling of loss, their writing then reflects the trauma that the self undergoes in the transformations of shifting locations and travelling across.

Emphasizing the impact of spatial dimensions on human experience, Edward Soja writes that people's ' "life stories" have a geography too, they have milieux, immediate locales, provocative emplacements which affect thought and action' (139). Diaspora, exile and forced mass displacements in the colonial regimes have led to the forms of writing that are intimately related to geographical consciousness and experiences. Soja says further that individual is not alone, the 'social order of being-in-the-world can be seen as revolving around the constitution of society, the production and reproduction of social relations, institutions and practices' (147). Literature's greater proclivity to place the individual within the quotidian and contingent social world has always tried to portray intersubjectivities as moulding subjecthood.

Theodor Adorno in talking about subjectivity warns us against the notion of 'pure interiority' of self, devoid of any contact with external reality. He considers this to be an elusive idea, for he believes, as Martin Jay puts it, the search for 'a pure subject prior to mimetic behaviour would lead to a false infinity of desire for a reality that is as elusive as the Kantian things-in-itself' (Jay, 53). Sovereign individuality, as an original entity is only the result of a social division of social process. 'The human is, Adorno says, 'indissolubly linked with imitation: a human being becomes a human being at all by imitating other human beings' (Jay, 54).

An important aspect of one's self awareness is how others see one—the presence of the other frames the 'I' in a perspective, contextualizing one. These interlockings between the self and the other create tensions and relationships that much of literature tackles, as its focus is on single individuals, even when placed within well knit communities. Reflective consciousness penetrates into the ways of being formed and framed by others.

Constructing the self through one's narrative about the past events or through imagined beings are some of the modes of writing the self. However as many modes emerge through the works of different writers the analysis of both the process of writing and the focus on writing the self become meaningful to the literary critic. The essays included here take different angles, views and inroads.

U.R. Ananthamurthy's essay 'Writing the Self' (a slightly revised version of the Inaugural Address he delivered at the conference titled 'Writing the Self', held in 2006) makes wide-ranging references to literatures of various periods: Romantic, Classical and Modern, in India and Europe. He shares his own experiences as a writer and relates the individual writers to their immediate socio-political and cultural contexts. In periods of war or revolutions and national movements a writer sometimes becomes a spokesperson for an entire generation.

Autobiography fashions the writer's self, and claims authenticity. The autobiographical form which claims the most authentic and verifiable rendering of a life/self, may in fact show great diversity and ambivalent images, as each writer views the task of writing the autobiography differently. While one may be more focussed on events and social life, another writer may reflect and try to gain some insight into one's own life. In the essays by Uma Parmeswaran, Rajee Seth and Mridula Garg, each one an eminent writer of fiction, the autobiographical form is viewed from different perspectives as they look at the intricate intermingling of facts, truth and imagination in the making of one's own life's account.

Uma Parmeswaran, who writes fiction, poetry and criticism, thinks that the boundaries between fiction and autobiography often get blurred as the two overlap in an autobiography. Characters in fiction and the self of the author in an autobiography often cross borders creating a new image. She uses the Keatsian idea of the poet merging herself with the subject to see its applicability in this form.

Why does one write? What are the pressures in social or personal life of any individual that compel one to become a writer of stories and novels? In her essay titled 'Writing the Self: Intent and Content', Mridula Garg goes on to analyse her own mode of writing and then considers the problems a specially talented/challenged person might face in forming a self in a society emphasizing the uniformity of hegemonic thought.

In her essay 'From Being to Becoming', Rajee Seth opens by claiming 'I am at peace with myself', but her essay leads on to reveal the deep disturbances she felt within her formed by personal experiences as of historical events like the 'cataclysm of partition'. Writing has become an existential act helping her in formulating her self through it.

Dwelling upon the varied roles of a fiction writer, translator, poet and a critic Lakshmi Kannan reviews how the self gets new shades and depths with these in 'The 'I' of the Storm: The Self in Literature – Form and Trans-Form', The 'selves' created within her fiction are seen to be reflections of her own self by some readers whereas she as a writer aims at a distancing and detached relationship with the protagonists in her stories. An important role is played by the different cultural moorings of different languages, even though they may belong to the same nation, as she reviews her own experiences as a translator. Esther David, a sculptor who has taken up writing at a later stage, shares her experiences of the change of medium. In 'Words Liberate Me' she goes over her discovery of new aspects of her own self's ethnic and gendered facets.

In the second section of this volume, critical readers raise some different issues related to the writing of the self. The art of writing and its accompanying difficulties, the impact of social and community centred histories are seen by some, as are the impact of geographical (dis)location explored by some other writers. As one crosses borders and encounters different cultures what formations and reconstructions within the self take shape, are some questions that emerge in many of these essays. The essays begin with views about Indian cultural situations, and them expand to consider other cultural spaces. In 'The Difficulty of Writing/Reading the Self', Jasbir Jain analyses the twin aspects of the inscription and the reading of the self in literature. She puts together many of the texts that attempt to portray one single person, Mahatma Gandhi, who eludes a final analysis and attracts new insights; she looks into his autobiography, and the novels, plays and films based upon the multiple aspects of his personality. Jain examines the problems of creating a self when there is 'a fluidity (the aspect of evolving and growing) and mortality with its inbuilt erasures', which lead her to question the process of building up a self in novels from different cultural contexts, by writers like Caryl Phillips and Ramabai Espinet.

Harish Narang in 'Becoming Canadian, Becoming Indian: History, Politics and Ideology in *Maluka*' has explored the diasporic locations of S.S. Dhami whose work is rooted in personal as well as the entire community's experiences of displacement. He looks into the construction of the 'other', by such a writer who wades through prejudices of racial, ethnic nature.

That in the modern age identities are 'fraught with contestations of multiple agencies of nation, media and religion' has been argued by Sudha Rai in 'Beyond Purdah:

Intersubjectivity and Interstitiality in Imtiaz Dharkar's Poetry'. Taking several volumes of Dharkar's poetry for consideration Rai develops the evolution of the complex images of selfhood. Using postcolonial and poststructuralist theoretical frameworks Rai relates subjectivity to global mobility as seen in Dharkar's poetry.

Urmil Talwar's essay 'Childhood Ghosts and the Scars of Adulthood', discusses the relational formation of the self in George Lamming's *In the Castle of My Skin*, which she finds to be neither a confession nor an instruction for life, 'it is rather a reflection about life'. Her focus remains on the formation of the Afro-Caribbean identity with colonial encounters as she also carves out the shades of fictionalizing the personal history in the autobiographical form Lamming has used.

Another fluid narrative in which the narrator uses different voices to build up multiple possibilities of interpretation is used by Sudha Shastri in her essay 'Self/Selves?: Voice in the Construction of *Alias Grace*'. Shastri discusses how this novel is a complex construction of the protagonist's version(s) of her story that leads the reader to no final conclusion about the character and her 'facts'. Shastri examines the disjuncted self/selves within the narrative, creating epistemological ambiguities.

The reflection of Alice Munro's personal experiences in the stories and their characters invites several explorations in this volume. Bandana Chakraborty reviews the appearance of childhood memories of Munro in her stories and the use of the rhythms of memory in her essay 'Fictionalizing (Her) Self: Alice Munro's Short Stories'. The painful awareness that nags with a sense of failure is part of the process of growing up experienced by several young girls in many of Munro's stories. Nilofer Kaul's 'Unburying the Self: Confessions of Failure in Alice Munro' presents the sensitive self consciousness of failure in social success as moulding the selfhood of these characters. How far does this sense of shame and guilt derive from social pressures and in what ways does it leads to a stable, adult selfhood, is questioned by Kaul.

Preeti Bhatt takes up three Canadian short stories to relate the technique of 'focalization' in analysing the construction of characters' self. In her essay 'The Role of Focalization in the Construction of the Self: A Study of Three Canadian Short Stories', she uses the structuralist ideas of focalization to study the split and multilayered narrative voices within the stories that create a disjunctive and pluralistic story.

The sense of shame and bewilderment at a complex history of her family and community seen in Ramabai Espinet's *The Swinging Bridge* emerges from the character's attempted self-reclamation. Charu Mathur's 'A Narrative of Self-Reclamation: Ramabai Espinet's *The Swinging Bridge*' brings together history and family in the process of building up her own self.

Nidhi Singh in 'Interrogating the Arab-American Experience: The Novels of Diana Abu-Jaber' reviews the impact of geographical (dis)locations on the person's desire to reconstitute the cultural and ethnic identity. The ghettoization of the Arab-Americans in a migrants' marginal space creates many forms of tensions, enforcing a variety of hybridities. This essay, as some of the others that discuss works by and about displaced individuals and communities, examines the writing of the self from this point of view.

Writing the Self can also acquire therapeutic value as it helps the writer, and implicitly the reader as well, to examine the absences within one's life and its painful moments. Uma Mahadevan in her essay, 'Writing as Healing: *Unless* by Carol Shields', considers how Carol Shields in her novel *Unless*, works out a form of constructing a self through her act of writing, as the heroine of the novel reviews her own career as a writer. The self-reflexive process within the novel relates to the writer's own self. Mini Nanda takes another novel by Carol Shields, *The Stone Diaries*, where she deconstructs the complex web of memories in 'The Vagaries of Memory and the Shaping of the Self: Carol Shields' *the Stone Diaries*'.

Santosh Gupta's 'Self within the Shadows of History' considers the strong impact of the colonial rule and the anticolonial struggle of the Indians and the Burmese during the ninetieth and twentieth centuries. The emergence of alternate non-conformist selfhood lead one to raise questions about the sources of revolt and selfhood through political activism.

These essays reflect diverse viewpoints and interpretations of the literary constructions of the self. Well-known writers and critics have put forth their considered opinions on the significant concern about selfhood. We hope that these essays will generate new discussions and ideas.

Several of the papers included in this volume were initially presented at the conference 'Writing the Self: India and Canada' organised by IRIS from 22 to 24 February, 2006, in Jaipur. The focus of the conference was on the creative and critical perspectives of writing the self, in its autobiographical, biographical and fictional modes. Diasporic, national and dislocated experiences were some of the contexts of these explorations.

On having decided to publish some of the conference papers, some other scholars and writers were requested for sharing their views. We are grateful to the writers who have contributed their very valuable experiences and ideas in their papers. We thank all the contributors for their learned expositions and having been patient with us, as the volume has taken some time in making its final appearance.

Our gratitude to Professor Jasbir Jain, Director IRIS, is immense who first formulated the theme at the time of organising the conference and for generously entrusting us with the editing of the volume. She has been keenly involved in shaping this volume and has given us the benefit of her tremendous experience.

It has been a pleasant experience to work with Pranit Rawat and his team who have cooperated cheerfully in bringing out this volume.

REFERENCES

Adorno, Theodor W. *Minima Moralia: Reflections from Damaged Life* trans. E.F.N. Jephcott (London, 1974) pp. 152–155. Quoted in Martin Jay 'Taking on the Stigma of Inauthenticity: Adorno's Critique of Genuineness'. *Journal of Contemporary Theory* 23 (Summer, 2006), 54.

Merleau Ponty, Maurice. *The Phenomenology of Perception,* 1945. London: Routledge and Kegan Paul, 1962.

Said, Edward. *Reflection of Exile and other Literary and Cultural Essays*. New Delhi. Penguin India. 2001.

Sartre, J.P. *Being and Nothingness*. 1943. Eng. trans. H.E. Barnes. New York: Philosophical Library, 1956.

Soja, Edward. 'History: Geography: Modernity' in *Postmodern Geographies: The Reassertion of Space in Critical Social Theory.* London: Verso. 1989.

Section I

Reflections of the Creative Self

CHAPTER 1

Writing the Self

U.R. Ananthamurthy

I want to start my speech with a broad remark; I can think of myself, my identity, either as a 'self' or as a 'soul'. If I think of myself as a 'self' then I seek fulfillment; if I think of myself as a soul then I seek liberation from the bondage to 'this worldly' pursuits.

In India you have both these searches. A search for fulfillment would mean this: all my hunger for the experiences of this world, whatever desire is there, be achieved in this life; alternatively, If I think of myself as a soul I don't have to live all my life in a perpetual cycle of desire and disillusionment. A moment can come, unexpectedly, or by 'grace', when the illusory nature of hope-despair cycle becomes apparent and I am released. Ramana Maharshi said, when it happens to you, you will realize how simple the whole process is, for it could have happened any time in your life. W.B. Yeats desired both fulfillment and release and made great poetry out of the quarrel of both in him (Europe vs Asia too in some poems).

I must also add this to what I have said so far. I find it very difficult to find in my language (Kannada, in which I write) the two words which can demarcate self and soul, because both self and soul are called *atma*.

But the problematic (perhaps unavoidable) gift(?) of modern western literature to us writing in the Indian languages

Revised version of U.R. Ananthamurthy's Inaugural Address delivered on 22 February, 2006 at the IRIS Seminar, Jaipur.

is that we have got the notion of 'me' as 'self', in opposition to the notion of 'me' as 'soul'.

That is point, number one.

The second point I want to make is this: even in western literature, when I was a student, as I grew up, and started writing, I was a great admirer of Shelley. Tagore had also liked Shelley. Shelley had seemed like an *Advaitic* mind. For instance, my teacher, who was a student of Leavis, condemned the poem: 'Ode to West Wind', and said that Shelley was self-obsessed and sentimental. He was very critical of the famous line in the poem: 'I fall upon the thorns of life, I bleed', I said no—for it seemed to me that Shelley was only bewailing this *avatar* of the *atman* as a corporal body, which is an impediment to the great knowledge of Oneness with the Universe. So 'I fall upon the thorns of life, I bleed:' meant for me 'God liberate me from this body—so that I may merge with the universe'.

You have a Walt Whitman too for whom the self is something that merges with the whole universe,

Or let us look at some other great lines Shelley wrote when Keats died, 'Life like a dome of many-coloured glass, *stains* the white radiance of Eternity'.

These lines were very fascinating to me as a student, because life 'seems' beautiful, for it is *maya*. It is 'Life like a dome of many-coloured glass'. In both of its senses it is 'stained'—beautiful, yet a hindrance. It doesn't make you see the white radiance of Eternity.

This is almost a Shankara kind of statement or Upanishadic. *Maya* makes this world seem beautiful.

Now I am trying to recall my student days, that moved me greatly, moved me also in opposition to my fascination for Shelley and Advaita. Keats wrote in a letter that this world is like a 'valley of making souls'. I may not be quoting him correctly for I am speaking from memory. Alternatively, you can talk like Wordsworth; I came into this world a soul, 'like trailing clouds of glory do we come From God, who is our home'. In the process of growing up in this world I am covered with illusion, and hereby I have become a 'self'.

What do I think now?

I am more with Keats than with Shelley, more on the side of those who seek fulfilment.

Many of the writers belong to that kind of a mindset.

And there is another dichotomy: The self in the creative process—How does it participate in creation? Eliot had a theory about it and it is important for us to note that this was in opposition to the Romantics and Victorians and somewhat closer to the ancient aesthetic theory of our country.

The personal Self is only a catalyst for him. The catalyst does not undergo any change but it makes change possible. It speeds up the creative process in the poet. So he developed a theory of 'impersonality' in art, which sometimes came very close to our great Indian aestheticians, for whom without a *vibhava* there is no creation. *Vibhava* is the 'Objective Correlative' of Eliot.

That is one way of looking at all literature and again in opposition to it, whom do I think of? I think of Blake. Blake, I may not be quoting correctly, again—I remember he said 'this is mine, yet not mine.'

Jasbir Jain used the word 'authenticity',—now, the notion 'this is mine, yet not mine,' brings in a quality of authenticity to what one writes. Since what I write is mine, it is authenticated. Yet, it is not mine only—not just personal—it belongs to every one else. I would incline more to the Blake's kind of definition of the involvement of the self in writing.

As a fiction writer let me share another experience with you. It is a great accident of certain times that the self that writes is not just the personal side that writes. Historically some conspiracy would have taken place, I am calling it 'conspiracy' in quotation, For, by some accident of history, what I think of as my self is just not of my own self.

I may still be writing what I think of as my 'self'. This is what happened in English literature when D.H. Lawrence wrote

Sons and Lovers. I was a student in England in the 60s. I had a teacher who became a dear friend, Martin Green, and another teacher, Richard Hoggart, he was from the working class. If Richard Hoggart would write his own autobiography, I imagine, it would come very close to *Sons and Lovers*. especially in depicting his relationship to his own mother, his mother who sent him out to bring cigarettes (she bought cheap cigarettes which she kept in an impressive expensive pack).

There is a certain kind of earnestness in those who come from the lower classes. If you come from the lower classes, then you have over-earnestness, and an embarrassment that comes from that over-earnestness. All that you find in Lawrence and Hoggart.

Those who read *Sons and Lovers* in the 40s and 50s, I think of the working class intellectuals, young people, the large number of people produced in the red brick universities, secondary schools; there was a little revolution in England. Lawrence wrote the self in *Sons and Lovers* which was not just the self of Lawrence. It was the self of the innumerable young people who were coming up in life across class barriers.

It happens to certain works. I would say in my own writing in the late 50s and 60s, I must have produced a few things in my own language which became the self of many people. This must have happened to Nirmal Varma; this must have happened to many writers in India. But it is not done deliberately, it just happens accidentally, from good luck, otherwise if you have a very peculiar, singular kind of self and you write that self only; then you overpsychologize it, then it becomes a 'case history'.

Therefore, here is a danger of writing about the self; it can become an interesting 'case history'.

In many of the novels which are about 'growing up', where you have a disturbed self, even in a comic novel like *Huckleberry Finn*, and a lot of Dickens where the writing the self can become writing about the culture, contemporary problems of the time, the result is sheer magic. It acquires effortlessly sociological, political significance too.

Which is that American novel; I forget the name that had created so much interest ... where a teenager writes ... Yes—*Catcher in the Rye*. Look, you know—when I became Head of the Department in a Secondary Teacher's College, a Regional College of Education, I devised a syllabus that included a lot of novels on growing up. I thought if someone is going to become a teacher they should read novels about growing up. I had *Catcher in the Rye*. It transformed all my students, the whole class was radically influenced; they became more honest, more self-searching, more aware of the inner life.

In India the only virtue is obedience. If a student looks very obedient the teacher thinks the student is very good. If you are obedient your Head thinks you are very good. *Catcher in the Rye* changed all that.

I'll present to you one more idea, and then I'll stop. When times get very troubled, like in the 1930s in Europe, where you feel that my self in whatever form it writes, has no significance at all, because Hitler was rising to power with hypnotic mob fury, there was madness in the air, evil and racial hatred all around. In such times you tend to feel your self has no significance. At such a time Christopher Isherwood said, 'I am a camera, I am not a self, I'll just capture what I see with my "passive" self'. A great man like George Orwell, who had an active self sometimes as a political activist, felt helpless as a novelist, and said: let me just watch and record what is happening around,. If you read his *Wigan Pier* or his great book on the Spanish Civil War you see journalistic writing becoming creative.

Even Malraux did that But the interesting thing is that the camera also chooses an angle. It chooses an angle, you pick-up this rather than something else. Even camera can write a self but the self is not as actively engaged as in Blake,

Take two poems: Blake's 'London' and Eliot's *The Waste Land*. Eliot's *The Waste Land* is in the other mode, where the catalyst self is working, putting things together, whereas in 'London', 'When I roamed from street to street' the self is involved and its a great poem. Its a little poem, but it's a wasteland he is describing (I owe this insight to F.R. Leavis).

But the interesting thing is that Blake like all the prophets said that an angel dictated it to him. But we should not forget that Blake took care to correct what the angel had dictated.

Thank you. The self is still there.

CHAPTER 2

From Being to Becoming

Rajee Seth

Never had I thought that I'd be a writer. No such ambition was I born with. Nor did any sneaky desire for seeing my name in print ever rise in me. They say that if you are endowed with a writer's vision, you are a writer without writing. True or false? I don't know. But how can one reach others without expressing or conveying oneself? I do not know. What I do know for certain is that even in childhood reading and writing were my ways of spending the long summer holidays, the silent hours of the evenings, the vigils continuing deep into the night. Solitude has never been unwelcome to me. By nature I have been drawn to solitude, been self-contained and shy.

No questions arose within me either at the life that came to me. I have always held that we have to bring order into whatever kind of life falls to our lot and make it livable. It is an inescapable, existential rule of our lives, and no quibbling or fooling around is possible here. Only after accepting this ground reality does the business of attending to calling or vocation arise. This doesn't mean that my bents were vague or faceless. But I could never school myself into making them all-important, at the cost of tearing myself from my kin and context, and living only for myself. This has never presented itself as any option to me. May be because of this belief, even after becoming a full-fledged writer I never learnt to live life on my own terms or conditions. I am mostly at peace with myself. This peace could be termed a suppression of self by feminists. The charge would never be acceptable to me. For me, my composure stood for something over which my inner being could never ride roughshod.

What I definitely felt then was that within me was a vast, formless and opaque haze that I could not fathom. A fierce restlessness gnawed at me to dive into it, tear it apart and see it with clarity. But I was not able to do anything to quench this intense desire. I did not even know if this was a part of my own self or of something outside me. To know I would have had to go down to the depth of self-analysis which is neither easy, nor always possible. And nor is it certain that a person undertaking this exercise would stay as detached and objective as required. What I'd felt continually since the onset of adulthood was that within me lay a cry of distress, ever ringing. I had always felt that I was not a complete, integrated and cohered person. I was not complete or cohered in spite of my faith in values like honesty, sincerity, humility and compassion. And I also kept feeling that there did exist a place where such a state of unalloyed purity, of synthesis was present. What this place was, in which direction it lay, I had no clue to. Nor, if there was a way by moving along which a person could spare himself anxiety or perhaps self destruction.

This kind of disquiet is usually entwined with memories of childhood. It pushes a person towards things not attainable in the day-to-day world. But nor are they attainable to even the persistent seeker, unless the search is made more acute, the pain more painful. Despite being alive to this imperative of intensified search, there was no chance whatsoever in my life for nursing or nurturing this pain, this search.

My life has never seemed to me a continuum. Rather, it has seemed divided into two distinct segments or phases. The pre-writing period, and, the post-writing period. A reason for this sense of divide could be that the texture of the two segments was and is different. The first stage was one of tremendous difficulties and conflicts. Not the kind of difficulties or conflicts which, in the language of feminism, can be called pure feminine angst. Nor were these difficulties that are politically correct, and further, the cause of feminism or promise the pleasures of independence later.

My difficulties were different. They were connected with the tumults and turbulence being undergone by my parents, brothers, sisters and other family members. After the cataclysm of partition, they were forced to find their feet again, make life worth living on a new geographical space, amidst a different culture and different manners. None of us thought in terms of 'to each his own'. We, so to say, cried and laughed collectively. We were happy or unhappy as a body at not getting this or that thing. Our parents, on their part, never cried at their lot, nor taught us to cry or lament. For them it was no great feat or act of heroism losing all in the battle of freedom. They never became abject or craven, were never bonded to pity. Nor did they teach us to become so. Thus, lots of uncommon things happened in our family: such as the girls turning out educated in the full, modern sense of the word and the boys remaining practically devoid of formal education. The girls have got good grooms and homes, wealth and standing, but in the lives of the brothers and their wives things have not taken a turn for the better to this day. Grandchildren from the daughters' lines have traveled overseas and got a taste of foreign climes. But grandchildren from the son's line have not been able to un-moor themselves from the backwoods of small towns. Living and sharing the same parentage such disparity of fortune can make you feel guilty about your own life of comfort. The effect on the psyche of a woman growing amidst such contrary surroundings is worth thinking about.

It is sixty-two years since independence. Up to now nothing like a parental home has come up for us. My sisters-in-law have evolved a life of respect, standing and status without riches. To date the pitted earth and tottering walls around which my father's family pitched camp when they set foot on non-Punjab soil, have not been made even or firm. The kind of woman that develops amidst such experiences needs no telling.

For the most part I have disliked talking about these things because milking your woes has become an industry in the world of letters: as if pain or woe was a thing-in-itself in the spectrum of emotions, unrelated to pleasure. Later on, of course, in living the life of a writer, the relationship with pain and suffering underwent a steady change, as it had to. It is so for every writer, not only for me. It was in understanding this that the poem 'They too suffered pain', took birth in 1975:

Pain they had too; I too.
Pain that rent, harried, haunted
Them. Me too
Fear, hate, grief, dread
They underwent.. I too.
Haps, mishaps, risks and shocks
Befell them. Me too.
My pain was deemed great
Because I had words,
the means of saying. The lack of tolerance
What wonder they are quiet
un-quiet.
Does a wordsmith ever endure?
For every pain he
Churns out a tome.

The writer confronts pain in his own way, aglow with the taste of liberation and the lure of immortality. He liquefies pain, digs holes in the hard crust of life, and pours the liquid into each hole one after the other. If I say that the collective consciousness of women engaged in writing can be read, objectively, in similar terms, I may be forgiven.

In narrating the second segment of my life, I am going to skip all those everyday, non-writing happenings such as acquiring an education, setting up home and hearth, and bearing children. These are practically the same in everyone's life. The out-of-the ordinary thing here is that for me the launch of a lifetime activity like writing did not take place due to any deep longing, any beckoning of a dream, any overwhelming call, any irresistible pull of the past. For me, my writing took place because of a sense of fierce ennui, depression, a sense of futility, and a killing sense of suffocation. My belief that no questions could ever be asked about given destiny and about existence was wearing thin. Questions on these very things began to torment me. I desperately wanted to know, was there something else in the world that was bigger, stabler, firmer and of more substance than our existence and our little package of abilities? What could it be that was assailing my hitherto unquestioned self-containment, and further scattering my scatteredness? Where and which way lay the roads that made null and void the pangs of existence?

Buffered by such questions that rouse a ruthless, stubborn resoluteness in the icy sway of negation, I began again my disrupted studies—some twelve years after marriage. Sitting on class benches with young and fresh-faced girls clad in skirts and frocks, I became the butt of their teasing, made quarry by the age gap between them and me. For the first six months my self-confidence was at rock bottom. I felt that my understanding and thinking had certainly deepened, but that my ability to retain things in memory had thinned. The history of English literature seemed to me written not in English but in Latin or Greek. Later of course everything fell in place. I was certain that the kind of intimacy and interiority there was in the study of literature, its capacity to absorb originalities, was present in nothing else. Literature in any form is never inert and shorn of values. The grit and determination that came to me later to regard as invaluable every experience of mine or others as invaluable probably came from this inclusive temper fomented by literature.

I recall that on the night before the morning of my final paper in M.A. Part Two, high with fever I turned out some twenty poems. That was when I caught a strand of truth about myself, that I was most at home in the world of letters. This, and nothing else, fell in the ambit of my mind. From childhood to this day I have not wanted to settle for anything other than reading and writing in my personal time. If my snippets, diaries, epistles, poems, pen-portraits and essays did not emerge in book form it was probably because to be seen in print never occurred to me. And when it did occur, it was like a boat lying moored for years in loose sands, suddenly splashing full tilt into the waters.

My first story came out in 1974 in *Naya Prateek*: the second in *Vikalp*, then in *Dharmyug*, then in *Kahani*. To a greenhorn writer, what it meant to get acceptance and accolade from Agyeya, Matiani, Bharati and Shripat Rai need not be said. Born in 1935, I was nearing forty at the time, laden with a trunk-ful of conflicting, overlapping experiences into which it was hard to find order.

I have always tried to get my themes away from myself. But my close friends swear that in every work of mine I get placed in there, occur there. Who doesn't know that any piece of writing is an outcome of the play of the writer's conscious/unconscious? To fathom this, the pages of my writing are there now, like open cards. Feminist discourses have always labelled this effort of mine to keep my themes off my self as a kind of self-censorship. I would neither agree nor disagree with them completely. What I think is that one who writes sublimates pain and channelizes grief. As I said earlier, she makes a tome out of every grief. Once you've gained liberty of expression, your censors are no longer the same. But over and above all this, your personal life that painfully takes shape from a host of difficulties, is no public square open to all. Your life has a sanctity of its own. It is no amphitheatre where people give themselves the right to interrogate you at will. The writer has no doubt a commitment to people, but not at the cost of privacy and personal space. These are, however, questions of a different kind, and at this point can be kept in abeyance.

For a woman to start writing is like passing over to another stage of life. Here, others see with surprise a different you emerge from your familiar mould. They feel cut up at not finding a place for themselves in the new sphere come up round you. Writing is an activity where you need time, and time with creative possibilities. You need yourself for yourself only. You need to have a perspective on the world outside, and you need to be fully concentrated within. Closed space and trapped air suit no writer. Even in those areas of life already taken care of, problems come up. Soon you begin to understand that for writing you don't need any great war fronts or battle grounds. Family and milieu are in themselves big battle grounds that send buzzing the tiniest cell of your being at the least tug, so you are never really left to yourself. All your energy can be frittered in insulating yourself and making your milieu agreeable. It is at these moments that I feel that the epicentres of daily life that make a woman woman, have not changed one bit. I am certain that for a woman, being a woman is no obstacle in the way of her development. The obstacles surface from without, from outside. These are of the environment, of not finding time at the right time: not getting a writing-friendly corner to herself: on not being able to get across to those around her the real nature of the space and solitude she wants. The obstacles are also of time slipping from between her fingers, and failing health.

And above all, yet another world of letters awaits you, for you to cope with. It is, again, a world riddled with its own hang-ups, a world with tangles of its own. As your writing progresses you feel that a number of things are trying their best to trespass into the centre of your being. Your own family, the family of the family, and a literary family ever alert and on its toes to challenge each step of yours towards success and achievement. Despite all this writing does not cease. You have to go on once you have entered its realm. Once certain experiences within you are exhausted in writing, other experiences containing other shapes and patterns surface in the consciousness. Thus the process of creation goes on, giving you the illusion of limitless, unending creativity.

As for my own life, it has quite a few facilities to it. In the exacting discipline of becoming a writer my otherwise intolerant husband has been very tolerant and supporting. In a husband and wife relationship neither partner can easily stay with a writing mate, because the personal space of the writing and the writer, keeps getting eroded by the closeness of the relationship. The relationship in turn gets injured from the expansion of the overall space. It is a difficult terrain to negotiate. With the growing years as life takes away the qualities of affection, ease, sweetness and suppleness, writing generally is made the scapegoat for this state of affairs. Harshness grows between the couple. Difficulties increase, not decrease. From both sides mental violence increases. This can well be a theme for research in women's studies.

Like other couples of our age, we too have had our share of arguments, quarrels, disagreements, noise and din. But we have taken care not to wage these wars on the soil of writing and creation. When we do have to go at each other we still try to step off fixed positions and look at things in a detached way. It is probably a stiffer test for the ego of a man.

I do not wish for recognition and acceptance for reasons other than my creative effort. I have been a stern realist about my demands and expectations and have always put them on level with possibilities. I am beginning to know only now that I have been saved many pains, pressures, tensions, ambitions, compromises and lures, and that I have gained liberation from them, precisely because of this streak of realism. That the taste of liberation is heady and elating I came to know the very day when, sitting down to write, I felt the two halves of my life joining.

I felt that to grasp your whole self was nothing other than getting your mind, speech and action on one level. To recognize something bigger than your own self within your own life span is to recognize the face of dedication and surrender.

Jayashankar Prasad's *Kaamaayani* has been the world's greatest book for me. And as chance would have it, this very book I won as a prize twice in my school and college days. The reason why Prasad struck me as a devotee more than a man of letters, I understood when again and again I halted at these lines of his:

> Wisdom lies far, action elsewhere.
> Why would wish be fulfilled.
> The one not meeting the other.
> This is the tragedy of life.

I am held by these lines to this day. I have not lost faith in them. Whenever I have lost faith, it has been in my ability. Guillotined again and again, rolled in the dust of wretchedness, stripped of ego, I have returned to the same path again and agin, to the same odyssey of Prasad, of aligning mind, speech and action.*

---

* Translated from Hindi by Raji Narsimhan

CHAPTER 3

Writing the Self

Intent and Content

Mridula Garg

Broadly speaking there are two ways of writing the self.

First, a straightforward autobiographical recital of events as they have occurred in the progress of one's life, coloured of course by one's interpretation of the causal process. The dimensions of the canvas covered by the content can be different, depending on whether the focus is on personal events or on the larger social, economic and political milieu.

Second, one can weave a fictitious character around the knowledge one has of the self, garnish the events with a dressing of imagination, aided by memory and present it as a story, novel or drama. This fictional account will project the self, not as it was but as it ought to have been or might have been.

My assertion is that the essential difference between the two is more of intent than of actual content.

Fiction is the more honest of the two because of the simple fact that it accepts that the events, experienced by the writer in the personal or public domain have not only been reinterpreted but also fantasized. An autobiography refuses to accept that ego and angst play tricks on memory, colouring it with imagination in a manner so subtle that one can not be separated from the other.

In my role as a critic of my own fiction, I have strongly felt that any conscious attempt to write a true or honest portrayal of the self is self-defeating. Whether one paints oneself as a paragon or a pariah, there is bound to be exaggeration bred of familiarity, which is really another name for prejudice.

I would call an autobiography a dignified version of a confessional narrative. Most of the time, it is the literary form that crafts expressions of self-indulgence or self-laceration. One of the most celebrated autobiographies of the modern world is Mahatma Gandhi's *My Experiments with Truth.* Despite a perfectionist's laudable and largely successful assay at honest and unbiased rationality, it is still heavily loaded in favour of exaggerated self-laceration. Lesser works by lesser mortals tend to sway between self-glorification and self-abnegation, without settling down to a proper sifting of fact from fiction.

Two qualifications need to be made here.

When I say that autobiographical accounts are coloured by the individualistic interpretation of the causal process, I do not imply that textual historical writing is totally free of this malaise. Far from it. We are all familiar with the adage that history is always written by the victor, that is, it is written from a particular world-view or that it mirrors the writer's viewpoint or interpretation. Still factual events play a far more pivotal role in the writing of history. The simple reason being that however slanted or biased their inclusion or exclusion may be in it, the choice of events can not be wholly arbitrary. Since it can be exercised in a far more arbitrary manner in an autobiography, personal opinion can and does take precedence over facts.

Autobiographical accounts by fiction writers tend to be more flawed than those written by others. Fiction writing, by its very nature, requires that the writer fantasize his or her experiences. Having done that as a matter of course throughout the creative period, it is difficult to give up the habit of a lifetime when he or she comes to write an autobiography. Most writers settle down to writing an avowed autobiographical account after reaching ripe old age, to call a spade a spade, when they find themselves unable to cull the passion required for penning a work of fiction. In any case, they would have already used up the most momentous and dramatic events in their fictional work.

The autobiography is usually a pale rehashing of the events with more scandal value than meritorious purpose.

An exception to this may be seen in case of autobiographies written by first generation writers like the dalits in India or the blacks in America. A few first generation women writers may also be included in this category. They would be the ones who write an autobiography before assaying any fictional work. The character of the work would be closer to a first novel by a second or third generation literate, non-subaltern author, who drew heavily on autobiographical material but was averse to writing a straight life story. The reason could be self-censorship or ambitions of renown for creative penmanship.

At the risk of ruffling some feathers, I have to assert that the great flurry of autobiographies written by young women, which has appeared in recent times is very largely influenced by the market's demand for voyeurism. The women are, I guess, largely incompetent or unwilling to pen a work of fiction.

As opposed to autobiographical writing, creative fiction becomes possible only when the self rises above both indulgence and laceration to take on the mantel of an impartial bystander. It is not easy to distance oneself from the emotionally assailed self, and assess its actions and feelings as an unbiased spectator. But who said creative writing was easy!

We must remember that the creative process is primarily a search for a craft to express the experienced world and its fantasized re-creation in the form of a story, novel or drama. In the absence of craft, we would at best, relate our experiences as anecdotes and memoirs. A story or any other genre of fiction is crafted/created when we go beyond the actual experience, mix it with other memories lying dormant, spice it with a fair dose of imagination and serve it as an experienced reality, more believable than the shallow reality around us. Since reality is always coloured by one's perception of one's life and time, fiction is more than a description of reality, it is also a critique. But the success of the craft lies in creating an illusion that it is only recounting life as it was lived or telling a tale, which the writer happened to see or hear. That is to say, the more a piece of fiction appears to be autobiographical, the more successful it is as a creative work. An autobiography, which presents itself as a truthful account of the life and time of the writer, is at best a masquerade.

To fully understand the relationship of writing to the self, we have to address two questions. What is the definition of self and why do we write?

In answer to the first question, I would say that the self is something which has to be discovered by each individual and may or may not be in accord with the general definition of what is normal. Unfortunately, normal is usually a synonym for pedestrian or commonplace. There is a thin line, which divides the unusual from the abnormal. The search for the self by an extraordinary person may lead him to discover himself to be either unusual or abnormal. I want to quote from the real life account of a gifted child called Dibs to substantiate this. His nonconformity and consequent non-communication with the commonplace outside world made those in authority declare him retarded or mentally challenged. He was finally able to worst the system with therapeutic help to realize his potential as a wise rebel. I quote the letter he wrote when he was 15 years old to a newspaper, from the book, *Dibs in Search of Self* by Virginia M Axline to substantiate my assertion.

> This is an open letter of protest against the recent dismissal of one of my classmates ... I am indeed indignant at your callousness and lack of understanding and feeling. It is whispered that my friend was 'suspended with dishonor' because he was caught cheating on examination. My friend said he was not cheating ... he was verifying a date—an important date in history—and since accuracy of date is essential to establish its very existence, then it should indeed be verified.
>
> I think you fail to understand the reasons why we sometimes do the things we do. Do you call it a failing if a person seeks to verify accuracy? Would you prefer that he cloud his honest doubt in ignorance? What are the purposes of examinations anyhow? Are they to increase our educational attainment? Or are they instruments used

to bring suffering and humiliation and deep hurt to a person who is trying so hard to succeed?

... There are things far more important in this world than a show of authority and power, more important than revenge and hurt. As educators, you must unlock the door of ignorance and prejudice and meanness. Unless my friend is given your apologies for this hurt he has received to his pride and self-respect and is reinstated, then I shall not return to this school this fall.

With sincerity and intent to act, I am,

Sincerely yours, Dibs.

There are two conclusions that can be drawn from this letter:

1. We have here a small child, diagnosed to suffer from brain damage because he sat mute and unmoving all day in the classroom, did not speak or communicate with anyone at home and had violent tantrums. If he could write the above letter, when fifteen years old, showing qualities of leadership, sensitivity, and new ideas, then we must conclude that the societal preconception of the self is flawed.

2. We cannot write about the self unless we can successfully answer the question: what constitutes the self? Is it the power or authority it wields and the conformity it shows to the dictates of power and authority, or is it the desire to question and ascertain the veracity of the reality?

There is no single straightforward answer. Different people have different perceptions about the self. One person may look inwards towards it, so that all external parameters are perceived to lie on the periphery and acquire substance only when they are internalized. Another may perceive the self as something formed and guided by the external parameters, that is, society, cultural inheritance and the prevalent ideologies and credos. He may approve or disapprove of them. He may probe the darker side of this wider self or seek to preserve the brighter aspects. In either case, he will define the self in relation to the external reality. All that we can affirm with certainty is that creativity is closely related to a search for the self, whether perceived as an internal or external reality.

According to the psychological theory of creativity, there are five independent dimensions of personality, namely, extraversion, neuroticism, openness to experience, agreeableness and conscientiousness. Of these, the dimension most closely related to creativity was found to be openness to experience. This very openness also puts creative people at risk of insanity. Several data and biographical studies have shown that creative achievement and insanity are related to each other as more than chance. In fact they may share the same genesis.

This very suspension of both dogma and disbelief, however, makes fiction best equipped to investigate the complexities and contradictions characterizing the self. The fictionalized account can address the demons and the pitfalls; the dilemmas and the indecisiveness as well as the spurts of energy and sublimation of the instinctive urges of the self because of the openness to experience, which is the definitive mark of creativity.

There is one challenge that all attempts at writing the self have to face, and that is of not keeling over to fall prey to the ever present threat of insanity. At least long enough to produce a sane piece of work. By sane, I mean a work that stands true to its inner logic.

This brings us to the second question. Why do we write?

One writes because one is not ready to accept the world, impinging on the self, or the self formed by the environment and the accepted value system at their face value. One has a vision of an alternate world, which is substantially different from the given world and in which, the self too takes on a different form.

I believe that fiction touches the commonplace with passion and turns it into art. It touches the tragic with the comic and reduces the bombastic to the absurd. It gives hope to the hopeless, goads the complacent to rebellion and generally plays havoc with the given ideas of right and wrong. It is therefore eminently suited to undressing, probing and dissecting the outer self to reveal the inner layers.

Some writers may not, of course, succeed in shedding the mores and prejudices imposed by the existing world and end up believing it to be the only reality. Once they take the reality as a given quantity, they would be satisfied with portraying the world and the self as immutable, unless outside powers, which are beyond their control, change the system. They would then use their writing prowess to try and preserve the reality in its pristine form.

In most cases, however, creative writing concerns itself with the need for change. This change, again, may be perceived either as a change in the self or as that in the external reality.

Realistic writing or reformist writing concerns itself primarily with change in the external reality. The writer is disillusioned not with himself but with others, who occupy positions of power and authority. He feels that the way to fashion a different world is by either revamping the establishment or by putting pressure on it so that it starts a process of change in the existing social mores, value systems and power equations. In both cases, change has to be brought about in the external environment through external forces. The self needs to change only to the extent of a deeper understanding of these external forces and for embarking on greater activism.

The other kind of writing, which leans heavily on an understanding of the psyche of the individual, proposes that change in the world is concomitant with a change in the self. It not only embarks on a search for the multi-layered, complex self but also undertakes to construct an honest critique, viewing it in the larger perspective of the external reality. Well, as honest as possible.

Disillusionment with the outer world remains something of a farce unless one is disillusioned with oneself to a greater measure. A truly great writing is one which effectively combines the critiques of the internal and the external selves.

Almost all fiction writers are amateur psychologists. They probe into the psyche of their protagonists, put them in unusual, demanding situations and try to chart their behaviour. Practicing psychiatrists may well balk at their attempts but I guess the writers can hit back by asserting that they may be technically trained but we have commonsense. After all, two of the most famous or infamous Freudian precepts, the Electra and the Oedipus complexes were first aired in Greek tragic drama.

What lends greater credence to fiction's assays in the realm of psychology is that instead of issuing linear or one-sided dictums regarding the behaviour of the individual characters, it leaves it to the readers to fathom a solution from a multiplicity of options. The actual solution is one favoured not only by psychological theory but also the author's philosophy of life. A case in point is the celebrated Hindi novelist Jainendra's *Tyagpatra*. The chief protagonist Mrinal, a newly-wed young woman confides to her husband about a pre-marital love, only to find that he gives a fig for honesty or truthfulness. Cast away by him, she goes to live with a lowly, uncouth and violent coal seller and gets pregnant. After the baby dies, she shifts to the slums to serve the outcasts and rejects of the land. When her well-heeled nephew comes to take her home, she spurns him, saying, 'Is your house big enough to accommodate all these outcasts? If not, I am not interested in going with you alone.'

The question which has exercised readers for a long time is: is Mrinal a masochist, bent upon self-laceration or an ascetic, full of love for the lowly and the poor, intent upon serving humanity?

We may well ask, if her object was to serve humanity, why did she opt to live with a boorish, uncultivated fellow? Did she have no other option open to her? We know she did. She was an educated woman, who had been a teacher. It was her insistence on telling the unalloyed truth, which got her in trouble each time.

Modern rationalist readers insist that Mrinal is a masochist, who has got into the habit of punishing herself because of the childhood trauma of getting beaten up by her sister-in-law for receiving a love letter. Others look upon her as a dedicated philanthropist, devoted to social service, a minor Mother Teresa.

The explanation may not be quite so linear. We have to go beyond psychological theorizing and refer to the author's world-view to find the real explanation. The common thread running through Jainendra's novels is that of disillusionment with the hedonist urge, that the only real freedom came from the renunciation of all desires. Since an ascetic wanted nothing, no one could exploit him. Since he had no desires, nothing could hold him in bondage. He was free forever of the tyranny of the market, the dominance of material goods, the emotional hold of relationships and the dictates of society. If we look at Mrinal from this standpoint, we have to concede that she is a woman of singular courage, who succeeds in discounting the mores practiced by society. In the process, she obtains a sense of complete freedom. She can in the end sublimate her personal renunciation to identify with the poorest of the poor. She lives with them and serves them, not from a sense of duty but as a fulfilling pursuit.

We find that the self has so many complexities and contradictions that it is not possible to see them all, if one is too close, as one is when writing an autobiography. Since creative writing depends in large measure upon looking at things from a distance, a novel can do far more justice to portraying the self.

In this respect, my favourite is Dostoevsky's *Brothers Karamazov*. The wide spectrum of characters, ranging from the lecherous Karamazov, the carnal Dmitri, the anarchist and intellectual Ivan, the half-witted Smerdyakov, the spiritual Alyosha, the ascetic Father Zossima, the earthy Grushenka, are all put in the writers' laboratory of human emotions, to help him reach logical and replicable resolutions. It is hard to imagine any of those characters writing an account of the self with even half the depth or incisiveness.

In conclusion, I repeat that the self is constituted of two layers of consciousness: internal and external. Internally, it is a complex and often contradictory mix of rational and intuitive persona. Externally, it is formed by an interaction with the historical experience, the collective memory, the social milieu and the value system. It is always a difficult endeavour to write of this self. But with all its limitations, fiction remains best suited to do it.

CHAPTER 4

The 'I' of the Storm

The Self in Literature – Form and Trans-Form

Lakshmi Kannan

> *'To speak is to be in a position to use a certain syntax, to grasp the morphology of this or that language, but it means above all to assume a culture, to support the weight of a civilization.'*
>
> —Frantz Fanon, *Black Skins, White Masks*

Literature is an arena where the 'Self' of a protagonist has a full play (I shall, from now on, free the Self from its alienating and cumbersome quotation marks and let it take its rightful place as a *person* in literature). How the Self is formed and how it gets transformed in its interaction with the environment, with situations and experience, more importantly, in its interaction with readers, seems to be an eternally nebulous process. Not just for the reason that the Self can take many protean forms, but more because of the dynamic and complex relationship that comes about between the Self of the protagonist, the more elusive Self of the author, and the Self re-created by the reader/critic/scholar. Together they make for a certain synergy in which Selves merge, submerge and surface in ways that defy any conclusive observation.

Inevitably, the Self is layered with the culture, the language represented by that culture and takes on the 'weight of a civilization' in the way only an emotionally endowed political philosopher like Frantz Fanon can describe. He could foresee that in the creative process of literature, the Self eventually becomes much larger than what the author envisaged it to be.

However, where Fanon at his point in time found that the Self in literature as something beleaguered by the power play of forces from the First world that surround literature from Third World civilizations, I find that the same Self has a strong, resilient 'I' that is culturally, nationally and sonically so distinct and intact as to earn my admiration for the way it keeps its shape and form despite all the political storm that blows around it. I also respect this Self for its valiant survival, notwithstanding the forces that try to belittle its dimensions. I hear the voice of this 'I' clearly, whether I am creating a protagonist, or whether I see him/her emerging in a book by another author. Storm or blizzard, the 'I' keeps its ground, because it is at once grounded in its roots even while it can soar beyond its roots, taking its author along with it very far, to realms that transcend narrow barriers of gender, to realms that melt the conventions of grammar on its fluid way.

And when the author decides to use the 'I' in a first person narrative, the dykes fall faster, for the 'I' can now take on such a force that it may be difficult to contend with. It seems to move on with a will of its own that the author could get carried away by the sheer urgency and immediacy of this 'I'. The reader too absorbs the narrative as something that comes with the credibility of a 'lived experience,' narrated by a voice. For an unwary reader and critic, the 'I' can be a misleading signal that makes him/her fall into the usual trap of inferring that the 'I' is the author's Self, and therefore, it is her voice. However, by a strange paradox, the very choice of a first person narrative can ironically give an author the distance and detachment that she wants. To her the 'I' of the protagonist is the voice of the *sutradhar,* the narrator of the story.

What I wish to share in the paper is the liberating experience of travelling along the Self of a protagonist in his/her own tortuous path in life, complicated by the language trail it travels through, from original Tamil, to re-surfacing in translation in other languages, and re-appearing in English language or in original English, and the colours taken on by the Self overseas, in an international or multinational context with the

Selves of other works that come with different colours and speak different languages.

The Self is manifest in poetry in a way that is very different from its manifestation in fiction. It pervades poetry as a dominant voice or mood, and in some of my poems, it took on the transparency and texture of water in its manifold forms as in a river, an ocean, a well, rainwater or just water in a glass on the table, for domestic consumption. I heard the voice of a woman in this Self, and I followed her as she dissolved in the various symbolic myths, legends and dimensions of water that form a cultural legacy for our people. I let her Self ripple her way through the shaping images and metaphors in ways that intrigued me both when I wrote and later, in her interaction with readers.

Every sensitive reader 're-creates' this Self for him/herself, till one can almost see another Self born out of this interaction. It will have a bit of the reader in it. The Self then becomes a voice that talks to the reader directly if tacitly, in the language of silence, in the very private exchange that a poem can provide a reader. It is easier for a poet to be carried on into an impersonal sphere in which the author feels her own Self expanding in inexplicable ways. She can understand the heaving energy of the tireless waves in her existence, or she could, for a moment, feel pure as the rainwater dropping from the sky just as easily as she could feel sullied by the dirt of living that even the great river Ganga cannot quite escape. She could well be the collective muffled voice of a historic gallery of gaunt women whispering to her in the *ghats*, the waters rippling closer and closer to tell her something that she was too afraid to hear till now, or murmur things into her ears that she could not/or did not want to believe till now. Poetry does the magic for her. And who is 'She'? She could well be Everywoman, manifest in the river, the ocean, the well, the water coalescing within her Self, merging with the elements.

When it comes to fiction, we immediately locate a cultural, regional and national context to the Self of the protagonist as it goes through the many fictions of self, manifesting itself on more tangible and explicit terms. When the chief protagonist is female and the author happens to be a woman, predictably some real or imagined connection is seen between the two, i.e., the Self of the protagonist and that of the author, although I doubt if one should make a special case for this. Why I dwell on the readers'/critics' response will become more clear when I move on to the Self of my male protagonists. All through my younger years, my young female protagonists were either supposed to be me or my camouflaged self or submerged self. And the two protagonists in my novel *Going Home*, Gayatri Shankar and Rama Doraiswamy had people speculating if Gayatri is closer to me than Rama or the other way around. One distinguished critic in Tamil Nadu declared that there is a lot of me in Gayatri, and that naturally makes Rama my alter ego, whereas the two are very different women with different experiences. As for all the protagonists featured in my first three collection of short fiction, namely *Rhythm, India Gate and Other Stories* and *Parijat,* they were all supposed to take off from my Self, whereas I have never been through the kind of lives they lived in the interior of Tamil Nadu.

The stories that appeared later in journals, magazines and books featured older women protagonists, and they were also promptly traced back to my 'Self'. During the same period I wrote as many stories with man as the central protagonist. Some were young, some old, some not so old. I felt rewarded by these stories because of the very positive response I received from readers and critics from a wide spectrum of languages, beginning with Tamil in the original and the translations in Hindi, English, Marathi, French and other languages. In all the critical discourse that followed, the absence of inference (as it happened with such monotonous uniformity with the women protagonists) struck me, because actually I had put in a lot of 'me' into these protagonists. I had also followed their struggle closely as they navigated their way through their complex lives. Moving through their evolving selves, their consciousness became mine, their emotions merged with that of mine and some of the choices they made were ones that evoked my empathy. More than the women protagonists whom I had placed in my early works within a narrow, regional context in which tradition and custom rules with an iron hand of patriarchy (something that I am relatively free of, in my own life in Delhi), I now identified myself closely with the travail, problems and the existential situations the male protagonists found to find themselves. The more the senior men cogitated about mortality, about the imminence of death, extinction, irrelevance, the transience of life, the death of the loved ones and other end-of-life conditions, the more I related to them. Yet, in all the critical deliberations, there was an unstated but clear-cut distinction made between the Self of the men in the stories taken as exclusively 'male' and my Self as a woman author. Therefore, when many readers/critics observed that I have 'remarkable empathy' for my male protagonists both young and old, and I was asked. 'Just how could you imagine their feelings so accurately?' I did not know what to say.

For me, the Self is definitely on an androgynous plane. For them, it was still a gender thing, while for me it was something that went well beyond gender. If I tell my readers that I identify most with that unnamed, old man in the story 'Nandanvan' in English and Marathi translation and *Jab Dharti Nandanvan Bani* in Hindi (*Nilam Nanadavanamanapin* in original Tamil), the man who can communicate with birds, squirrels, plants, flowers and trees, and that all of them 'talk' to him in a language he understands, they are not very convinced. Likewise, if I tell them that I identify the most with the old man who travels alone by the tube in London and sits around in various parks in the story 'Savvyasachi Square', (*Savvyasachi ka Chauraha* in Hindi translation, and *Savvyasachi Chadukkam* in original Tamil) or with that middle aged man who undergoes a near-death-experience in *Aakash hi Aakash* in Hindi translation ('*Engum Vaanam*' in original Tamil), I get the same response. Similarly, I could identify a lot with the younger men in my early stories—Ramachandran in 'Please, Dear God', the man who watches his wife wasting away in an ICU of a hospital on an indefinite coma and fears that she may die; Sukumaran in 'Zeroing In', another young man who is tormented by his 'temporary appointment' in a government organization that keeps renewing it after every two years; Ganeshan in 'A Writer Proletariat' who questions the very relevance of writing *per se*; and Rajaraman in 'The Maze', caught in the corridors of power where a jungle law rules in a ruthless corporate world. People wondered about how I wrote about them and had me thinking about the thing called 'Self'. So where is the 'Self' that we seek to identify in all its transformations, I wanted to ask. Is it encased within a narrow definition of gender? Is it trapped within the form of a story or a poem, or is it something that breaks through these barriers to grow and outgrow its initial limits and merge with the Self of the reader? Does it not have a life beyond the book or the story?

What is far more important than the question of the author merging with the Self of the protagonist is the dynamic exchange between the protagonist and the sensitive reader. The stories with male protagonists drew the most positive responses from readers, particularly the male readers. The stories brought out the submerged 'selves' of the readers to the surface, and they emerged as a layered entity that absorbed myths, legends, fables and the cultural mores of their background. It was interesting to see how they could enrich the story outline with their 'selves' in more ways than one, and how the stories 'completed' their sense within them. In effect, it also completed the symbiosis of creativity for me, because I have always believed that a story/poem/essay finally completes its meaning only in the sensibility of the reader.

The Self in literature also has a lot to do with the tangled issues of language. As an expatriate Tamil writer based in Delhi, I choose to write in the *nom de plume* 'Kaaveri'. The minute I take my Tamil 'pen', I sense a change that comes over me. For one thing, it transports me to another region—Tamil Nadu and its various cities such as Chennai, Madurai, Trichy or parts of Karnataka that could include Bangalore, Mysore, Shimoga, Tumkur and so on. When that happens, my protagonist also changes. She is this person who 'belongs' to a culture and *yet does not belong* in many ways. Rather, she is alienated from her culture, but to know exactly how she is alienated, I need to place her, first of all, firmly within a cultural context. Only then would it be clear to me—or to the reader—where her Self is dislocated from the social milieu within which she lives, and towards what direction she seek to move on. Therefore, she often comes through as an identifiable Tamil woman but one who does NOT wish to walk the trodden path of her community. She may have her reasons.

Naturally, 'acceptability' and 'approval' becomes a debatable issue here, so she, the protagonist, the story, and by oblique reference, me (as the author) go through various stages of rejection, acceptance, recognition, inclusion or exclusion in anthologies, in research studies towards Ph.D. or M.Phil. or M.A./B.A. syllabi. The roadblocks that one hits here are definitely gender-specific and culture-specific. The Self of the protagonist has to take a chance with the gatekeepers and custodians of 'the great Tamil culture' who keep a vigilant watch over the 'image' of a Tamil woman. Yes, they represent the moral police amongst the male judges as well as the female judges who support patriarchy for their own benefits. I was informed by two women, who submitted their Ph.D dissertations on my fiction how contentious their defence of their thesis turned out to be in their viva, with certain male examiners angrily questioning the stand taken by them (the Ph.D aspirants), by the protagonists in the fiction and by me, the author. The younger of the two women described it as nothing short of a battlefield.

The same Self of the protagonist undergoes some transformation when the story is published and read in its English translation. She is then on an equal footing with many other women from across the country, and that is when she is seen from a broader perspective. It is interesting to watch how the Self of female protagonists caught within the repressive, traditional and conservative norms of a Tamil society are in some ways 'liberated' through translations in English, or in Hindi and other languages. Their anguish or pain does not register in their own milieu in quite the same way as they do in another language. Things come through to the Hindi readers with either a new perspective, or one that strikes a chord in them with the feeling, 'Ah, that's how it is in our community as well.' As for English, it gives a wonderfully neutral ground to any work and gathers such a wide range of readers from a diverse background that the protagonists stand a good chance of receiving a non-judgmental, liberal evaluation that is in sync with the contemporary times we live in. Gender inequity, gender bias, the closed mind of a community towards tyranny practiced in the name of 'custom and tradition' and the puritanical way in which the same community can clamp down severely on feelings related to love, attraction, sex or a sensuous appeal—all of them come for a re-view. In English translation the Self of the protagonist sheds the weight of her culture for a moment. While translations into Hindi and other Indian languages, at their best, have a textual fidelity and an effective transfer of ethnic elements (because one can find analogies and parallels for almost everything), English takes the work on to a different plane altogether. If the Self of the women protagonists in the Tamil original showed them as 'trapped' in a repressive community until they make that choice or effort to break free or re-arrange their lives to find their space, the English language 'worn' by the same stories at once shows up her background as unchanging or slow to change, or just downright retrograde and the women as being at variance with the paradigms of their community.

Where the senior male protagonists are concerned, each one of them has a Self related to many people from across the country and overseas, in trans-national forums. I could not have created the senior men of the stories around them if I was not totally involved in the process of their evolving Selves that pass through phases of doubt or fear of a loss of the very Self that we are talking about. I could make them real to the readers only by understanding their anxiety about getting 'unreal', I could make them visible only after understanding their fear of becoming 'invisible' to their family and people with every passing day. They had to first of all 'live' for me if I have to understand the strange thrill some of them felt about the imminence of death and the promise it held for liberating their Self. I worked my way through these paradoxes to catch their evolving persona.

On the same league as these men is Muniyakka, the old maid who winds in and out of three of my stories, but with a difference. She has a healthy cynicism that gives her a wacky style of living, and her nonchalant, devil-may-care attitude gives her the strength to live absolutely alone in life, taking each day as it comes. Muniyakka and my male protagonists took me to a plane of consciousness that is far above the consciousness of the young women protagonists who were so zealously identified with me by readers.

Going back to English as a medium, conversely, even translations in English or original writings in English are defenseless against the possibility of being thrown-back to their 'regional' slot when it comes to readers from overseas or when it comes to an international scenario. When a work shrinks into a 'regional' slot, the Self of the protagonist also shrinks in proportion in the eyes of the readers. The 'cultural nationalism', as Aijaz Ahmad pointed out in his book *In Theory* (1992), has a pervasive consequence. In order to see how anything that is 'regional' gets relegated to a minor status, one needs to recall what he wrote: 'This is not the place to review the complexities of this situation, but there has clearly developed, in all the cosmopolitan cities of the country, an English-based intelligentsia for whom only the literary document produced in English is a *national* document; all else is regional, hence minor and forgettable' (75). The Self in a regional literature has to necessarily become 'small' enough to throw in relief whatever is written in a dominant language. Nothing reaches the Anglo-American academy as easily as

English. To quote Ahmad again about this imbalance: 'The upshot is that major literary traditions—such as those of Bengali, Hindi, Tamil, Telugu and half a dozen others from India alone—remain, beyond a few texts here and there, virtually unknown to the American literary theorist … . One consequence, then is that, the few writers who happen to write in English are valorized beyond measure' (97).

'Politically, we are Calibans all,' declares Ahmad about literature of the Third World (102).

Two years later, Homi K. Bhabha in *The Location of Culture* (1994) talked about Fanon and how 'His (Fanon's) existential evocation of the "I" restores the presence of the marginalized.' While recalling the position that Fanon took, Bhabha remarks: 'It is a painful re-membering, a putting together of the dismembered past to make sense of the trauma of the present'.

With that, we come full circle. The Self in literature has to take the entire weight of a civilization if it has to come through as real. The way this civilization, culture, nation or region is made out to be problematic by Anglo-American academy, or Western and Westernized academy is hardly the problem of the Self. It will continue to stand in its lonely height, the more distinct for its 'difference', the more recognizable and therefore tangible in its alienated position in the larger picture. It has an eloquence even when it is silenced. And it does not have to go searching for imagined homes, for it is already housed within the readers.

In the creative process, the 'Self' develops, gets moulded, and just as easily it also gets submerged. The 'Self' of the author gets submerged in the complexity of the creative process and it may get buried somewhere between the 'Self' of her protagonist and her own, unrevealed self. At any rate, where the writer happens to be a woman, the trajectory of the female 'Self' goes through a path that could cause much contentious debate at times. More than two journalists who interviewed me for the media regarding my novel *Going Home* remarked with surprise that the writer Rama Doraiswamy in the novel 'is not like me', and why did she continue within a marriage that was clearly a disaster? Why didn't she walk away from her insensitive and jealous husband, wouldn't I have sought a divorce in my life if such a thing happened, was the question I was asked. I had to tell them that Rama indeed is a very different person, at which point they again asked, why did I create a woman protagonist who is otherwise an intelligent, qualified professional and a successful writer, but who goes through a meaningless marriage just for the sake of appearance. My answer that there are women like Rama did not seem to satisfy or convince them.

The 'Self' as we understand it, is transformed in the process of creativity till it reaches a point of objectivity in the eyes of the author, and perhaps the reader. The creative process gives an aesthetic distance.

He or she. That is where the crux of the matter lies. Because he/she is not just a decorum in communication that we have woken up to recently in deference to the gender sensitivities of the present century, it goes far deeper when you set to analyse this elusive thing called 'Self', be it the protagonist's or the author's. It gets deeper and more complex when the author happens to be a woman, or the protagonist also happens to be a woman.

Things get far more complicated when the various forms of 'Self' are seen against a wider, general context or in an overseas programme in which English as a language of communication dominates. English and the vernacular instantly get polarized, and that further deepens the way a 'Self' is received or interpreted by the readers or audience. Things are at once taken as 'regional', or 'national' or 'international' on very common arguments. Some major regional writers who have an international reputation are averse to the comment from Western critics that their books are 'national allegories'. This is a narrow slot to fit a book in.

REFERENCES

Ahmad, Aijaz, *In Theory: Classes, Nations, Literatures*, Oxford University Press, 1992. First published by Verso, 1992.

Bhabha, Homi K., *The Location of Culture*, Routledge: London & New York, 1994.

CHAPTER 5

Words Liberate Me

Esther David

My world has no definite boundaries.

Because, as a student of art in the early sixties, my guru told me, 'Just because you are a woman, never use the word sculptress, because you are a sculptor.'

Since then, I appear to break barriers, whenever I felt that being a woman was an encumbrance. I strive to be myself, a person, a writer, and I do not want to make an issue about being a woman writer. I do not like the word *authoress*, in the same way that I do not like the word *sculptress*. For example, if my work faces criticism, I take it constructively and do not assume that I am being criticized, just because I am a woman. It just happens to be that, I am a writer who is a woman.

Although, I often write about women and there are a number of women characters in my books. This happens because I understand female sensibilities better than anything else.

For example, in the seventies, as a sculptor, I was not conscious how the female form started emerging in my work. I made a series of sculptures in wood, based on the theme of transformation and my sculptures represented woman as bird, fish, tiger or snake.

I used to carve in rosewood, because I liked it's warm glow and fragrance. Sometimes I also carved in teak wood, as I liked the grains, which flowed on the surface of the sculptures and the wood carvings became fragile and weightless.

But, in the eighties, I realized that I was imprisoned in the blocks of wood and only words seemed to liberate me. Sculpting was becoming a burden and I did not want to be a sculptor anymore. I wanted to reinvent myself with words, with a voice of my own and in full control of my creativity. I was not at peace with myself.

I tried to find comfort in books, because much before this turmoil started, I had already created my own literary world, in the library of our ancestral home in the walled city. Here, I had three storytellers feeding my imagination, the library where I read all that I was not allowed to read, my grandmother who told me family stories and Mani, the cook, who regaled me with folk tales.

Mani was an uneducated widow, but had a sense of humour and a rare facility for words. As a writer, I was always searching for Mani in the women I met in the slums of Ahmedabad where I introduced Art for Development with various organizations. This experience took the form of literature. *By The Sabarmati* is dedicated to Mani and the women who shared their stories with me.

Interestingly, Mani often appeared in my novels, like this: 'She lets me watch while she puts on a freshly washed sari and also permits me to look into her tin box. It has a broken mirror, two saris, a torn petticoat, a multi-coloured poster of *Kaaba*, and a small wooden perfume box lined with velvet, holding a little cut glass bottle of jasmine *attar*, the only remaining keepsake to remind her of her family. She opens it and allows me to float in the fragrance for a moment, and then closes it again. There is no reason to wear perfume. Tobacco is the only flavour she knows. It deadens all pain'.

For years, I did not know the meaning of my name.

It became the reason for the search of my Jewish ethos, hidden somewhere within me and waiting to be discovered.

This search drove me to write in my first novel *The Walled City*: 'I want to ask him from where we come and where we go. We do not know from where. But we know why. From sure death. Expulsion. Exile.'

While writing, I also noticed that my Jewish experience started seeping into my work. I wrote in *By the Sabarmati*: 'To me, her sorrow was almost holy, like an old Hebrew scroll at the synagogue, kept behind a curtain in a vault that faced Jerusalem and the Wailing Wall'.

I understood that my Jewish experience was hidden somewhere within me and waiting to be discovered through my novels. This search drove me to write *Book of Esther* and *Book of Rachel*. Slowly, it started seeping into my work. But, I did not want to understand it through religion; instead, I started a personal research through the study of Jewish history and family histories, which gave form to my novels and a new dimension to my life.

CHAPTER 6

Writing the Self that Isn't, or Not Writing the Self that Is, Boils Down to the Same

Writing the Self is What Each Reader Sees in It

Uma Parameswaran

I write this as an author of fiction and poetry, not as a scholar of critical methodologies.

We usually make a distinction between autobiographies and memoirs on one hand, and fiction/poetry/drama (or creative writing as I call it) on the other. We associate truth with the former and fictionalizing/romanticizing with the latter. The line is a lot more blurred than we assume.

Fictionalizing is always present in the confessional mode, whether it be autobiography, memoirs or letters. The writer shows only what he/she wants to show. The moment one puts pen to paper, or finger to keyboard, in modern parlance, imagination and objectives takeover, and inscribe what the writer wants to communicate to the reader. An autobiography might be factually correct about such details as dates and places and the external identity of people, but actions and relationships are twisted, distorted, manipulated, to give a certain viewpoint—literally the position from which the reader is made to see the event or persons being talked about. The writer may not be aware of the colouring he/she gives to the reading of characters and relationships, but the intrusion of the present self is there in the selection, sequence and discreet interpretive signatures of the details. In other words, the autobiographer does exactly what a fiction writer does—manipulates the narrative to give an intended effect.

In creative writing, fictionalizing is more clearly on the surface, but surely there is something of the author or poet in the characters or personae beneath the surface.

I do not pursue the confessional mode in my creative writing. My own credo comes from the Keatsean concept of the poet as chameleon, a creature that takes on the colours of the surface on which it runs and has no colour of its own. I do not encourage students to identify the speaker within the poem with the poet himself but always to use the term 'persona' for the speaker. If the persona in many different poems express the same sentiment or ideology, I say, then and then only should we attribute to the poet any of the values or ideologies one sees in the collection. This puts on the reader/critic the responsibility of reading extensively of the writer's output, and not to depend only on anthologies.

In any anthology, bear in mind that the editor plays a bigger part than the poets in how the poet is perceived. For example, I published a volume of poetry, *Trishanku,* in 1988. The collection consists of about fifteen different voices articulating different aspects of the immigrant experience. There are several poems in the collection which speak about racism against non-whites in Canada. Editors of anthologies have consistently selected these poems. Since anthologies seem to have more circulation than one-author volumes of poetry, readers tend to assume that the personae in these poems are to be identified with me, and this misleads a reader, who often enough becomes a published critic, to infer that my main theme is about racism. The poems where I celebrate Canada are seldom noticed. Also popular among editors are my poems where the persona speaks in broken English, and thus the editors perpetuate the notion that immigrants come with a poor knowledge of the English language.

If the same thought, imagery, or experience recurs in a writer's oeuvre, as I said, one could rightly speculate that it is close to the writer's heart. Even so, I say, 'Do not assume that the experience being spoken about is autobiographical.' This reminds me of another problem with anthologies.

An editor once phoned me to say that she was interested in the poem from *Trishanku* 'where you talk about your father.' This completely confounded me. I have only one poem in the collection which comes close to autobiographical, and that is about my mother who passed away very suddenly on the third day of Navaratri of a certain year. It is in the male voice of Chander, one of the main characters in the cycle of poems, and it fits just right into the narrative that follows Chander recalling his early years in Madras/Chennai to his present life in Winnipeg as a professor in a science discipline ending with a dilemma he is facing at the time. The poem that this editor had in mind is in the voice of a boy, Dilip, who remembers his early boyhood when his father was his hero, 'And in the winter/he'd walk on the water, my father', and who is now in a more materialistic world of keeping up with the Jones', and has a huge, seldom-used boat in the backyard of his house on the riverfront (itself a symbol of wealth and of 'having arrived').

Back to Keats's concept of the chameleon poet. Elsewhere, he expands his credo further, to explain how a chameleon poet is not merely one who mechanically transfers colours from one medium to another but personally participates in the process, absorbing the colours of the medium-subject so that he becomes it. He speaks of becoming one with the sparrow that he is watching one spring morning. So, the chameleon becomes one with the medium-subject on which it runs in order to communicate the colours. The experiential aspect is essential for subjective poetry, whether it is personal, vicarious or imaginary. For the period of poetic composition, the poet becomes a full participant in the experience. A whole lot of screening, censoring, exaggerating and pruning take place consciously or subconsciously, and the final product might be a far cry from the original experience, but in the process of editing, something universal is enclosed in something particular. For example, a poem might, in essence, say something about life, death or love, but if it is subjective poetry, this is said through specifics, through the birth of a particular child or death of a particular friend. The child or friend might never have existed, but for the space of poetic creation, they are real to the poet. If the poet succeeds in making them real, however momentarily, for the reader, the poet should be fully satisfied.

That is what creative writing is all about—becoming one, albeit for a short time, with the persona within the poem, and if the poet can make the reader feel one, albeit for a short time, with the persona, the poem can be called a success.

Wordsworth talks about what the chameleon-poet does when he explains the apparent contradiction between his two major phrases about poetry being 'a spontaneous overflow of powerful feelings' and also 'emotion recollected in tranquility'.

This process of feeling empathy with the persona (in a poem) or main character (in fiction) often leads the writer into serendipitous insights.

Much of my fiction published to date is a retelling of a story that has been told to me or has happened to someone around me. I have duly acknowledged most of the sources on the Acknowledgement page of each volume. However, the story that I have written may not exactly be the story that the storyteller told me. Be true to the story, says the old narrator in Isak Dinesen's 'The Blank Page'. There is a Native Canadian tradition that not only should one acknowledge the person from whom one 'received' the story but also that one should not change a word of it. While this injunction could be considered in respect of all oral literatures (which is why our Hindu epics survived so many centuries,) writers usually take liberties. However, the criterion is the same—are they being true to the story? As readers, we have to make the judgement call, and we often don't. Consider, for example, the current assumption among westernized scholars that all versions of the *Ramayana* should be given equal status, even those versions that make Ravana the hero and Rama the villain, or those that persistently read Rama as a misogynist etc. These writers, clearly, do not remain 'true' to the story, and critics, by allowing them space, do little justice either to the epic or to critical scholarship, let alone any justice to Hinduism. I have appropriated friends' stories, but I trust I have not misappropriated them. I would like to include one example of the serendipitous insight.

The title story of my *Fighter Pilots Never Die* (2007) is set in Winnipeg and opens with Latika hearing over a phone message that her husband had a stroke on the tennis court and has been taken to the hospital. On the way to the hospital, she thinks of her youth in India and how she was wooed and won by a fighter pilot. The plot is built on a story told me by a friend—that she was once married to a bomber pilot in the Indian Air Force, who died in the 1971 Indo-Pak war. It touched me, and became a source of the story. I did some research on the historical aspects of that war, and also freely fictionalized my friend's story. I showed her a draft of it before its publication, to make sure there was nothing in it that would offend her. She phoned back soon after, and said she appreciated the way I had built my story around the power of memory and how memories are always with us, even when we are not aware of them. She said that recently, thirty years after the 1971 war, she had to undergo a surgery, and the friend who was by her bedside when she came out of anaesthesia told her later that the first word she uttered was the name of her first husband and not of her present one. On reading the story, casual readers might think it odd that anyone would think of one's first husband when the second's life is in peril, but there are psychological connections that are obvious to a careful reader. However, what really pleases me is that my friend's anecdote about her surgery shows real life vindicating my imagination!!

Writing is often like camera-work—the angle, the aperture, sharpness of focus, the play of light and shade, all are important. You can sometimes get by, by using a lot of colour to make up for lack of focus. Sometimes, you can purposely shake the camera for a blurred effect. Modernists often do, to show the chaotic aspect of life, but good writing has to have a basic coherence even when depicting the incoherence of life. I leave readers to make the final judgement on my novel, *Mangoes on the Maple Tree*. Several readers have asked me if I had a sequel in mind since the novel 'ends abruptly,' as one put it. The novel is about an Indo-Canadian extended family in Winnipeg, and each member has an almost equal amount of centre-stage time. Each member has a problem, just as about everyone in the world has. Three of the major characters in the story arrive at a resolution to their problem, but the fourth, Jyoti, does not, in that she does not quite choose between her two lovers. The novel is as complete a story as any one would find in any family. While there is nothing of my own personal life in the novel or in any of my writing, there is something of me in every character, and that, after all, could be called 'Writing the Self'. The chameleon, it seems, does leave its own imprint on the medium.

One of the exercises I give my creative writing students is to make them guess the line in a classmate's poem that they think started the poem, and then check with the writer as to the correct answer. For poems often start with a phrase or a line that starts pecking like a woodpecker at one's brain. One such line was 'seduced by false reasoning accept and spread their lady's creed', around which a poem in Chandrika's voice was written (in *Trishanku*). That was my reaction to the company of a group of delegates sponsored by the Government of India who had come to attend a conference in Mexico City in which I presented a paper. There was also a young poet from India, who was looking for ways to emigrate to Canada. It was the time of Emergency, and the jargon of the government delegates made me think of many normal intelligent citizens who too had succumbed to the superficial lure of how trains ran on time and bribery and crime had decreased.

But let me digress into when and how I wrote the poem (I am a writer, remember, and there is always some degree of fictionalizing in all that I say). I was on a breakfast flight back from Mexico City. The Mexican airline, like Air India, had rather attractive frills, like an artistic menu card. On it, I saw all kinds of authentic and appetizing Mexican foods but when my tray was served, what did I find but brown bread, grapefruit and yogurt? It happens every time you ask for a vegetarian meal—you are handed an invalid's diet, while your fellow passengers get to tuck away scrumptious hot food and chocolate pastries. I expressed my disappointment to the flight attendant, especially since everything on my neighbour's tray was vegetarian, and she made the usual apologies about catered food and how nothing could be done. So I nibbled at the brown bread garnished with a sprig of parsley and lettuce. A few minutes later, the flight attendant returned, with a tray full of Mexican dishes (from the first class section, I presume) and a bottle of Mexican wine, given with the airline's compliments. After which the Muse took over. Now that is a good story about poetry-writing, don't you think, and also tells you why one of my favourite stories is Gloria Sawai's 'The Day I Saw Jesus on my sundeck ... .' about a prairie woman in Moose Jaw, Saskatchewan, who, in order to postpone the chores of a Monday morning, sits on her sundeck with a glass of wine, and gets to see Jesus come by for a visit with her. Keats would have thanked the invisible wings of poesy, and not the wine.

I could tell a similar conception or gestation story for each of my works, but that is enough for now. In short, there is no need to write one's own story when the stories around oneself and in one's imagination are so much more interesting. I have to add an anecdote or two about the way I am, the way many of my generation have been brought up. At an academic feminist conference, a Chinese colleague presented a fine paper, with very relevant data and logical deductions. The moderator, in her summing up, duly complimented the presenter, and then added that she would have liked to see the presenter putting more of herself into the paper, more personal details and views, a more 'feminist' manner of presentation. I was quick to protest, pointing out that some of us had grown up with the ideology that one, male or female, never spoke about oneself, and we were also taught not to think well of those who did.

I had a colleague whom I used to meet at conferences on a regular basis. We had long chats, not only about the papers presented at various sessions but about her cat, her furnace that had to be replaced, the courses she had to teach, her current male friend/s, travels she had planned .... One year, the conference was at my university and I was the main organizer. My husband had come to help me out with some chores and I introduced him to my friend. She turned to me and exclaimed, 'I've known you for ten years but didn't know you were married!!'

So, though no doubt my creative writing is replete with references that can be interpreted with the theories of Freud and Jung, Derrida and Lacan, Kristeva and Dworkin, I shall leave it to the reader of my fiction and poetry to figure out those complexities. One such reader is an imaginary character in my as yet-unwritten novel, who has long planned to write a critique of my works from the biographical and psychoanalytic critical perspectives. This character will expatiate on a great many speculations(cleverly disguised as analysis in incomprehensible critical jargon) on the many images that bare all the minutiae of my life story, my dreams and nightmares, my oppressions and suppressions, and make it a 'grand' lurid saga of sex and violence that will become a best-seller.

Section II

Critical Explorations

Section II

Critical Explorations

CHAPTER 7

The Difficulty of Writing/Reading the Self

Jasbir Jain

Caryl Phillip's *Dancing in the Dark* (2005) opens with the sentence, 'If you walk down Seventh Avenue today he is a man who never existed' (3). A man who dressed well, walked tall and was watched by men and women alike—yet a man who has, in every possible way, ceased to be. *Dancing in the Dark* is about racism and identity, and raises certain issues regarding the processes that go to make the self. The external pressures are many—birth, economic location, national or diasporic location, the way one dresses and carries oneself, relates to other people and the profession/vocation one follows or is compelled to follow. The moment one examines the implications of the word 'writing', other affiliated issues come forth. Writing is a 'mark', it is a 'character' (character in the sense of a letter or a sign), often the word *inscribe* is used, as for instance, 'inscribing a self' that leaves a permanent impression. Then how do we reconcile it with fluidity (the aspect of evolving and growing) and mortality with its inbuilt erasures? How can one resolve the tussle between the need to change and the need to remain the same?

The interrogatory exercise that I have chosen to undertake is a kind of thinking aloud, it seeks to problematise the ways in which selves can/cannot be written, the processes that are adopted along with the challenges that need to be met. My examples will be drawn both from autobiographical and fictional constructs as the two genres display different structures—autobiography is a framing of the self by the self and is always in process; fiction is, in many ways, more finished and objectively framed. At one level fiction, because it is a long narrative, is a good working base for theorizing the writing of a self. The writer uses his position very much like a creator. And when the characters make independent choices then they sidestep the authorial impulse, bringing in the unconscious and the uncertainty and unpredictably of action. All these traits are clearly manifested in the biblical story of Adam and Eve.[1] But the moment we refer to the Bible, theology comes in. The self then is immediately cast in the mould of the religious faith it has inherited, and which becomes a guiding force both in its making and its interpretation.

Contemporary psychology has provided multiple frames: there is the psychotic which works through obsessions; the schizophrenic works through division and alterity; the sociological rationalizes through the theory of roles and games people play, that is, it stresses relationships and the presence of the other, while the moral works through a relationship with the self.[2] Yet these are a person's immediate and close web of factors; over and above this there are the larger, often abstract, concerns like nation, ethnic identify, race—colour of the skin—and its related stereotypes like 'coolie', 'nigger' and 'yellow', coloniality and economic subjugation.[3] How and in what manner can or does the 'self' negotiate these constructs? Further, one needs to identify the counter-claims of these categories vis-à-vis the individual self.

The self-in-the-world is not a simple equation between two entities. There is a whole set of intervening factors and concepts that have emerged in the last century on account of large-scale migrations, globalization and independence movements, which threaten the old fashioned concepts of the integral self. Instead we now have hybrid selves, hyphenated and twice hyphenated identities, multi-layered and multi-generational identities, fragmented and transformative selves not necessarily simultaneous or linearly developed and chronologically located entities, but scattered, circumstantial and confrontational. The self, in the actual act of literal writing, is often written in another language, a by-product of colonialism and migration.

Coming back to the process of writing and its fixity, there is perhaps a need to look at it in two different ways. The process can be viewed as a continually unconscious one, reflected upon retrospectively or summed up by others. It is rarely a self-review, not even in autobiographical writing. And the process, in itself, comprises of orality. I am using writing in a double sense—as effectively bringing a self into being and projecting it, and as the act of recording and portraying it. Of the two, the first is of greater significance and most of the traits I have been discussing belong to the first category; the second becomes a public act either through performance or the literary act indulged in by the individual/writer. The two acts of recording may be separate or overlapping. The performative action through which the self comes into being may be observed and evaluated by others; it may also be accompanied by letters, diary entries and public statements that debate the conflicting elements as in the case of Gandhi. Shift this to the creative work, of a writer who in the act of writing reflects also his self; a study of the writer's oeuvre opens it out to the reader. Often we refer to it as the writer's world-view. The fictional work captures the debates and conflicts of the writer's mind even if there is a dichotomy between his personal life and the imagined world. I am thinking of writers like George Eliot, especially with reference to *Felix Holt,* the fact of social ostracization, the question of legitimacy, the self-enforced exile and the return to a situation of power, all of these somewhere articulate Mary Ann Evans's questioning of these issues as they affected her life. Placed outside the normative patterns of moral behaviour, George Eliot's work is a continuous debate between the intentionality of the individual self and the social judgmental frame imposed on it. The conventions of interpretations are constantly being challenged.

Autobiography and Imagined Reconstructions

M.K. Gandhi's *My Experiments with Truth* is a writing of the self in the literal sense. In fact, Gandhi wrote his self in different ways and the dominant one is action. The formal recording of this action—the need to act, an examination of the propelling force, the moral conflict, the choices made, the emerging strategies—are all reflected in this self-assessment which came out in 1927. All along there are two time scales: the retrospective look bestowed upon the past when Gandhi is in his mid-fifties, more than half way in his political career which was to end in 1948, and the actual period lived across several decades and recording whatever memory had saved. The reader travels the same ground with Gandhi as he writes about his embarrassments, his fascination for new experiences, exposure to the West, loss of his mother, right through to his fatherhood, dietary experiments, public life and the vow of *brahmacharya*. The self comes through as an erring, stumbling self, learning from mistakes, with a penchant for taking vows and testing his determination through their implementation. Also as a person who weighs the consequences carefully, and strong-willed bordering almost on the dictatorial. The evolutionary process is a gradual one and the emergence of the later Gandhi is prepared through a constant fluctuation between vanity and withdrawal.[4] Three agencies—experience, analysis of that experience and the moral interventions in that analysis—can be identified as the determiners. None of the three is dispensable. If the South African experience is to be identified as crucial to the shaping of the Gandhian self, his early habits of analysing his actions (the logicality of the mind), evaluating them in moral terms (the pursuit for truth) leading to his tendency to seek non-confrontational, non-divisive and non-violent methods are all of significance. On many occasions Gandhi uses words like 'expediency', 'compromise' and 'negotiation'—whether it is with reference to Abdullah Sheth's case, some other legal case, negotiations with the South African government or later, with the British government. Yet all along he reveals an early abhorrence of cowardice as well as a determination to overcome it amounting almost to a public confession of his weaknesses and faults. He is equally steadfast on the question of principles. They are not compromised in anyway. There is a growing sidestepping of ritualized practices and closed structures like caste[5] and a decision to discard the sacred thread because it is one of the signifiers of caste (328).

Gandhi's autobiography moves constantly between the political world and the personal decisions necessary to support his stand. Throughout his inner struggles, prior to taking a decision, are debated. For instance, he discusses the concepts of *aparigraha* and *samabhava.* Regarding possession, he wonders:

> How was one to divest oneself of all possessions? Was not the body itself possession enough? Were not the wife and children possessions? Was I to destroy all the cupboards of books I had? Was I to give up all I had and follow Him? Straight came the answer: I could not follow Him unless I gave up all I had (221).

The solution was to choose a mid-course, think of himself as a trustee, to give himself to the community and widen the meaning of the word 'family'—thus rendering the personal into a category that embraced the non-personal.

The narrative is constantly interrupted by introspective reflections, self-critiquing, consciousness of criticism being levelled at his practices as hollow pretensions (234). It shows a continuous effort to work towards a non-personal model of behaviour where the evaluative principles are morality and truth. Yet, there must have been some moments of crisis which necessitated introspection and determined his code. Being thrown out of the railway carriage was one such, and being pushed off the pavement another. It is these climatic moments, public and decisive in the making of Gandhi, that have been singled out in the imaginative constructs. Richard Attenborough's film takes an overview of his whole life, centralizing his relationship with India; Shyam Benegal, using Fatima Meer's story of Gandhi's apprenticeship, works out the incidents that took place in South Africa. Other more literary forms like Giriraj Kishore's *Pahla*

Girmitiya, Partap Sharma's *Sammy* and Nand Kishore Acharya's *Bapu* reflect on the internal debates and are reflections on Gandhi in the twenty-first century.[6] Here too Sharma and Acharya deal with entirely two different phases of Gandhi's life, Sharma focusing on South Africa and Acharya on the closing years—the years of failure—1946–48. It is these two dramatic texts I propose to consider briefly to contrast with the autobiography, and bring out the difficulty of interpreting and reading a self. The autobiography, however, does not cover the period of Acharya's play. *Bapu* derives its material largely from history and Gandhi's letters, and knits the two together through a psychological re-examination of the past.

The fact that both the playwrights have chosen to strategically split Gandhi through the dialogic form, is a clear indication of the foci of these plays. From the external political events they have shifted to the mind of the man, and each, in his own way, invents different strategies to read and project the Gandhian core self. Sharma uses two Gandhis—Mohan and Mahatma. The older Gandhi interacts with his former self, laughs wryly at it, puts the self through a course of analysis and subjects his actions to retrospective scrutiny; Acharya uses the form of multiple dialogues embedded within the monologic form, discussing not through interaction but through recollection, filtering them through Gandhi's perspective. Both the writers in their reading and writing of their subject's self have also challenged normative dramatic structures in entirely different ways.

There is a tongue-in-cheek attitude in Sharma's play as he explores not merely Gandhi's mind but also the responses of people who had to put up with his eccentricities and decisions which upset their expectations from the system. Partap Sharma opens out those crevices which are smoothened over in the *Autobiography*. While Gandhi looks at the end result, the persuasion which has worked, Sharma looks at the doubts that assailed the minds of those who employed him, needed his services, consulted him and ultimately expressed faith in his leadership. But there are moments when they doubt him. Abdullah Sheth views him as another kind of headache.

Sammy is a play in two acts. The opening scene has Mahatma on the stage confessing loudly to his shadow existence. This is in the nature of a prologue and an Actor appearing on the stage, states the purpose of the play. Gandhi did not come ready-made for history, hundreds of smaller men had their share in the making of Gandhi. The Actor has an advantage: his very profession facilitates a crossing of all 'barriers and boundaries'. He is told, 'You have a chance to get inside other people, feel their skin from within. You understand the sufferings and conflicts of each persons, [...] even the aches in their bones' (6). Additionally, Sharma uses the transforming of roles strategy where the actor switches roles mid-stream. This particular actor plays six different roles.

In England Gandhi's concentration had been on western dress. In South Africa it was his Indian headgear and dress that become a source of identity. Partap Sharma's play has short, effective scenes that go on unfolding strategic decisions and place them simultaneously under contemporary and retrospective scrutiny. Constantly the actors stand outside their roles, acknowledge that they are playing roles, mock and laugh at each other and point out the strategic significance of every decision and action. First, race surfaces as a more significant marker than nation, then it is clear that religion is working as a separatist force, and later the role of political power as a controlling force stares one in the face. One by one, Gandhi confronts these issues in order to build a sense first of community, and then of nation. The Mahatma comments on Mohan's lifelong search for the purpose of his life, and Mohan on Gandhi's need to be 'fully naked in both body and mind' (12).

Gandhi's perceptions took shape through a whole series of confrontational acts—all of which turned him back to his own self and the need to purify and strengthen himself (35). The self thus is placed in a reciprocal relationship with the outside. There are moments of doubt and uncertainty, moments when the power of sheer faith carried him through (43). Correspondingly the justice of a legislated provision also stands exposed as discriminatory practices are legitimized. At one point, the Mahatma tells Mohan, 'You are trying to turn personal ethics into a political possibility. You are forging a new weapon' (44).

As the play progresses, solidarity emerges as another feature linking the outside world of politics with personal ethics. Bit by bit the structure is constructed—through dress, a shaven head, a sidelining of family interests, inter-dining and crossing the barriers of caste, class and religion. All along there is a struggle with prejudices that one has inherited, also there is a constant struggle with the ego, without which the self cannot emerge, and if it becomes overpowering, the self cannot grow. Public confessions, transparency in all thought and action are ways of putting back this ego into place (66–69).

The second act shifts to India and Gandhi's new political following. The incidents focussed upon are the moments of co-operation and withdrawal. Mohan is now the Mahatma—thus, the two have united. Time has bridged the gap, General Smuts is replaced by the Viceroy and new symbols like Khadi and the Charka are found. But briefly, the Mahatma makes a comeback as the voice of conscience in order to take part in an internal debate regarding the course of action to be adopted, carefully choosing between the intellectual and the common path. Ordinary skills that touch the common man's life like spinning and making salt are connected with the achievement of freedom—a foregrounding of the means to be adopted and the transformative change imperative in the human medium—for freedom to become a reality. *Sammy* works with both the moments of decision-making and the concept behind the political action. By locating the debate between Mohan and Mahatma, not only is the dramatic element enhanced but inroads into Gandhi's mental processes are worked out.

Nand Kishore Acharya's play is again a two-act one, set in two lonely locations—a hut and a room—indicating class differences. The sense of loneliness and a total sense of failure are sharpened by the presence of this single character on the stage. All other characters inhabit the imagination. Gandhi's dialectics are performed in memory. The time of the play is located in the forties, mainly 1945–1947. There is no journeying back to the formative struggles. What emerges are the Hindu-Muslim differences, the differing stands of the Congress and the Muslim League, and the sense of having been betrayed by his comrades in the struggle. Gandhi's perspective is entirely focussed on Indians as 'us', there are only marginal references to the outsider, the 'other'. It is a sense of defeat that envelops him, almost an attack on the very ego that he has been trying to contain all his life.

The political figures who are, one by one, placed in the dock are Maulana Abul Kalam Azad, the President of the All India Congress in the forties, Jinnah with his separatist demands, Nehru and Sardar Patel for their rigid stands. These leaders are guilty of all that Gandhi has held at abeyance—secrecy, lack of transparency, falsehood, staunch religious attitudes, personal ambition, leading to separist tendencies—and these cracks are symbolized by Gandhi's cracked heels with which the play opens.

Through this self and other examinations the history of the negotiations, exchanges and settlements, the closing years of the Raj are laid open. Letters that have been written, riot situations, disagreements and behind them the deep hurt of Gandhi as he is face to face with his own failures. *Bapu* is a sad play, tragic in its sense of erosion of values, and comes through as a turning point in the nation's history. Is the subject of Acharya's play Gandhi or the nation? Is it a retrospect of Gandhi's life or is it Acharya's view, himself a historian, from the standpoint of 2003 and the aftermath of this collapse of the moral structure with the entry of power? A recurring stress on the word *apne*, my own, lays Gandhi open to the charge of narrow affiliations. But it also transfers the nation to a filial construction—an old father, who is now dispensable, and his many sons squabbling for power, in fact a war of succession, no different from the one Aurangzeb fought with his siblings.

The play *Bapu* can be read in many different ways—a reflective play which needs to be told simply and staged austerely, a dialogic play which needs to be inhabited by living memories and hidden figures, a history play acting out the past, and a biographical play where Gandhi is nursing his hurt ego and analysing the past, passing on the responsibility of guilt to the others. It opens up the moral dimensions of both Gandhi and his political followers.

As one turns round the play on its axis, several questions crop up—how has the writer read Gandhi? And then, the Director and the Actor in their turn?[7] Further how have their readings *written* the Gandhian 'self'? In fact, the play raises questions of biographical writing. But before I turn to that, the possibilities of interpretations need to be addressed first, and an important one is in what way can Azad, Jinnah, Nehru and Patel be turned into active presences without giving them living roles? Is it possible to do it through language, sound or collages? Or newspaper cuttings or stylistic change? In fact, how is the internal conflict to be turned into a visible and a visibly audible one?

Both the writers base their plays on a selection of events, choosing to focus on different phases of Gandhi's life. For one the base is Gandhi's life, for the other it is history. The psychological reconstructing details the struggle but it still raises the question—is there a way to reach the core self? Or there is always a gap in the way we think of ourselves and the way others respond to us, interpret us and reconstruct the inner being? As the self takes shape, the relationship of the signifier with the signified grows a third dimension, which is the element that escapes the signifier.

Biographical Reconstruction and Racial Projection

Caryl Phillips, himself a Caribbean, constantly engaged with the process of writing the histories of the island black, has taken up the life of Bert Williams, a popular comedian of the turn of the 19th-20th century who, alongwith his partner, George Williams, created a stage presence for the African-American music and gradually moved comedy away from racial minstrel conventions to a more human style of comedy. The comedy act was both self-mimicry, and a racial representation, entirely two opposite things and the placement of the artists was wedged between their need to survive and their need to belong to a larger collectivity.

Biography is a writing of another's self and involves the double act of reading it and empathizing with it. Caryl Phillips' identification works through a racial condition, the working of a stereotype and the manner in which it relates to the mainstream 'other'. Bert Williams and George Walker, two black boys who came together to earn a living out of the 'obliteration' of their true selves on a daily basis, 'Fourteen hours each day in the California fog masquerading as southern or plantation darkies' or northern zip coons, rubbing shoulders with Gold Rush dreamers from the Latin, Asian, and European worlds whose own identities appear to breathe free in the misty western air (29). This act is all along very humiliating as they also have the coloured audience from whom they 'silently beg forgiveness' for the acts of racial vandalism that they commit. There is an external face working in opposition to the inner self: transparency and bridging of the two, which one is able to trace in Gandhi's case, are simply not possible here.

Bert and George are also opposites: Bert is tall and big, George small and suave, Bert serious and withdrawn, George, the optimistic one who has knocked the word 'defeat' clean out of his vocabulary (28). He is the funny man and Bert the straight man in the vaudevilles they stage. Later on, in their career together, George works against this total surrender to the stereotype and wants to make a mark; Bert, however, more steady, realizes the difficulty of opting out of it. As their career climbs from success to success and they make a trip to England with *In Dahomey*, they also sense an ongoing corrosion taking place in their inner selves.

The black man's options of employment were limited. The roles available were all subordinate, impersonal ones like a hotel bellboy, minstrel performers in self-mimicking roles or burden-carrying jobs. Circumstantial restraints have no control on one's dreams or ambitions. Bert dreams of the Caribbean, George dreams of striking a new note. They also dream of going back home rich and famous. As they enter into emotional relationships with women, their lives pull apart. George squanders himself as he does his money, picks up syphilis and fades into oblivion. Bert lasts longer, withholding himself from even his wife and continues to suffer the ignominy attached to self and racial mimicry.

The novelistic reconstruction takes up the racial history both at the economic and the personal level as the struggle with the colour of skin and the kinky hair are a lifelong problem. The black, in a white society, is made to feel conscious of his outward appearance and this consciousness attacks his sense of 'self'. Bert William's life is portrayed as one of withdrawal, loneliness and estrangement as he tried to sustain his inner dignity. The popular song that he was asked to perform everywhere was 'Nobody'.[8] At the end of the novel our sympathies are fully with Bert Williams; we as readers, seem to enter his dark room and his fading popularity and are left with a strong sense of tragedy. Rage is also felt at the cornering of the victims that goes on all over the world. It is the process that Phillips's adopts for his act of writing Williams's self that interests me.

There is an occasional shift of the narrative perspective as first person narration takes over and describes the inner struggle. Additionally there is a strong presence of the racial group: silent disapprovers like his father, who forced to listen to the popular comments and the black anger against his son, abandons his barber shop; through his wife who enters the premature role of Mother and is denied a communicative relationship; through the man's choices as he opts out of some engagements and persists in others; and there is the understanding that exists between the two friends despite their different attitudes and life-styles. Bert Williams comes across as a man who makes himself through opposition—a tight rope-walking as it were—through laughing at himself and hiding his pain. His dignity sits on him like a shield as he moves from stereotype to archetype.

Writing the Self through Lineage and History

Ramabai Espinet's *The Swinging Bridge,* almost a century after Bert Williams, offers a similar example of tight rope-walking,—once again an outsider, a Caribbean, and an immigrant. *The Swinging Bridge* is a semi-autobiographical novel working out the dual themes of immigrant location and ethnic origins. The writer herself does not acknowledge its autobiographical reflections, but as Indo-Caribbean-Canadian the negotiations are constantly with her multiple past. All along there is a third theme, both more foregrounded and less dominant than the others, that of gender. This contradiction exists because for the writer and for the development of the narrative, woman as subject is important, but gender is part of the larger, more comprehensive identities of the twice-immigrants. Espinet traces matrilineages, researches the histories of Caribbean revolutions and digs up the protagonist Mona's past through the papers in the attic of their island home. One of the several questions she asks is: how do women record their history? In the process of Mona's researches, the frames through which history and lineage are perceived shift, instead surfaces the history of women—subordinated, compelled to give up their hobbies and passions, kept in the house or turned out of it—of women living outside nationalities and inhabiting only a gendered world.

The novel opens with the statement, 'It is an untold story'. And then follows the telling of the story where Mona as the apparent subject serves as a cover for Gainder's control over the narrative as woman, wife and mother, and later grandmother, a woman who had carried with her, her passion for singing, her folk songs and *bhajans*, a whole living tradition carried orally across the black waters and transmitted these through narration, writing and memory, words, whether written or oral that, haunt Mona. 'Words', Espinet writes, 'are ghosts, ancestors on this side. They are not symbols. They are alive and sensate—full of flesh and stone and jagged edges' (5). They jog her memory as cultural narratives hover around her and tales of exile and banishment from the epics are repeated.

The 'self', both for Mona and Espinet, is being written through a journey into the past and a refusal to accept it simply as history. It is written through a going back to the island home and the dream she has of it when all the houses they had lived in coalesce into one space. The house symbolizes the continuity of the past into the present. The prologues that introduce each one of three sections of the novel continue an overarching narrative which happens to be Gainder's and interweaves itself with Mona's at the end.

Writing the self also implies learning a language in both its literal and metaphorical senses. When Mona needs to read Alice's record of Gainder's songs written in Hindi, she needs outside help—the other—and enters into a world of translation. The act of translation is literally a going back and forth, so characteristic of the act of 'writing' the self. For the self is primarily a self-in-the-world. Writing the self is a multi-layered process; it involves confrontation, investigation and a constant balancing. Mona, like Espinet, lays on another layer beginning from the middle point, going forth and returning back to 'unfold' the past in order to shape her attitudes and 'write' her self.

Orality and Writing

In early childhood Gandhi's mother told him stories, in later life he abundantly communicated with people through his articles and public discourses; religious discourses and myths, as part of an oral tradition moulded his ideas. Walter Ong in *Orality and Literacy* writes, 'Human beings communicate in countless ways, making use of their senses, touch, taste, smell, and especially sight as well as hearing' (6–7 quotes his own 1967 publication). He adds that writing enlarges the potentiality of language almost 'beyond measure' (8). But it needs to be noted here that writing is a shrinkage of the oral space as it fixes meaning and narration. Ong admits it to be an 'imperialist activity' (12). The meaning of the oral statement refuses to be fully captured by or contained within the written words. The *Gita* which shaped Gandhi's life first came to him orally, later he committed the verses to memory through repetitive recitation.[9] Still later, he constantly gave oral commentaries on it before proceeding to write down his explanations. *Gita's* advocacy of truth, non-possession and detachment, was internalized by him and acted as a guiding force in his decision-making.

Orality pushes one out into a world of listeners. Some of its characteristics defined by Ong are that it is close to the human life world (42); its conceptualization is more immediate, responsive and experiential; it also stretches across time with remarkable ease. In *The Swinging Bridge* the ghosts of words that haunt Mona and creolize her thought and expression, evoking memories are carried forth from India and their many transmitters are unknown and half forgotten. The *bhajans* that Gainder had sung were often created and passed on through oral transmission.

In *Dancing in the Dark*, Bert Williams's life revolves around the world of movement—the minstrel, the comedy-act, the vaudeville, performative ways dependent on improvization, folk culture and oral tradition. A counterpoint exists in his withdrawal to his study and the self he keeps private—which again is not a written one. Here one has to move on to the second meaning of writing, of leaving a mark, of growing, of interacting with space—vacant or otherwise—in order to go on living. The examples I have taken indicate that the propelling force more often than not is conflict, a resistance to external circumstances and their discriminatory practices which attack one's notion of identity and force one into a mould. Conflict has its base in questioning and the search for breaking open the mould whether it be one of religion, race or gender.

The self in the act of writing incorporates a certain amount of orality that envelops us in innumerable ways. While orality flows through memory, writing uses memory in an entirely different way. It goes back to recollection with a view to reducing it to order. It loses the spontaneity of the spoken word and is detached from the actual experience through its distance in time. The written word involves a restructuring and reordering of experience: how does it then square up with autobiography? Paul de Man in the extract ' "Autobiography" as De-Facement' believes that autobiography belongs to a 'simpler mode of referentiality, of representation, and of diegesis' than fiction (172).

Following Man's argument, one wonders whether there is a need to look even more closely at the act of writing. Is it expressive of a specular moment, of cognition or is it an impulse into which the act has to be moulded? I would like to place autobiographies in a slightly different frame and say: each autobiographer differs; it becomes important as to at what stage of life it is written and for what purpose; that one needs to examine its self-dialoguing and other-dialoguing in order to distinguish between confession, statement, recovery, self-critiquing, assessment and an analysis of how it has come to be what it is.

The degrees of difference between autobiography, imaginative and literary biographical reconstructions, fictional representation are of significance as multiple ways of 'writing the self' surface. The act of writing is simultaneously a reading—of the self, the past, history, experience, others and of political contexts. They are interpretative by their very nature and all interpretation has an inbuilt ambiguity. Neither writing nor reading really succeeds, in capturing the self, which eludes even the subject himself. The sheer complexity of the undertaking is frightening.

Endnotes

1. Adam and Eve having been placed in the Garden of Eden, gave in to the temptation of eating the forbidden fruit and were consequently exiled. Desire, disobedience, temptation, a psychological play of power all combined to lure them away from their designated home. The whole debate about freedom, free will and choice can be traced to this and is a working model of how the 'self' escapes the creator and is dependent on the doer's will in order to articulate itself.
2. Freudian psychology built itself around repressed sexuality and the ego theory and traced mental illnesses to these imbalances.

Post-Freudian psychology recognized the schizophrenic tendency, the early signs of which are perceptible in the theory of the double. A constant factor in these theories is the relationship to reality—the external world—and the snapping of the connection with reality. Placing their study in the interactive world of social relationships, R.D. Laing, Erving Goffman and Eric Berne, each in his own way, explored the dimensions of division, role playing and consciousness of the other. For more details refer R.D. Laing's *Self and Others* (1962, Harmondsworth; Penguin, 1969), and *The Divided Self* (London: Tavistock Publications, 1960); Erving Goffman's *The Presentation of Self in Everyday Life* (New York: Doubleday Anchor Books, 1959); and Eric Berne's *Games People Play* (New York: Ballantine Books, 1964). Goffman's work is a consideration of the 'way in which the individual in ordinary work situations presents himself and his activity to others, the ways in which he guides and controls the impression they form of him, and the kind of things he may or may not do while sustaining his performance before them' (Preface), thus drawing attention to external signifiers and interaction. Berne developed transactional analysis, placing the individual firmly in a social set-up.

3. These are terms that frame a whole community and are indifferent to individual traits, terms related to coloniality and indicative of a preconceived prejudice.
4. See *Autobiography*, 43–45.
5. For more details refer to *Autobiography* 'wife is not the husband's bondslave' (21). Shyness helped him in his 'discernment of truth' (53), confessions to his landlady (56), learning the insignificance of dress from Hemchandra (64), being thrown out of the carriage at Maritzburg (93), arousal of the feeling of 'national self-respect' (117), compromise on the issue of wearing the turban (123), not acting as an individual but for the collective interest (163) etc.
6. *Pahla Garmitiya* (Hindi. New Delhi; Jnanpeeth, 1999); *Gandhi*, Director Richard Attenborough (1982); *The Making of the Mahatma,* Director Shyam Benegal (1996). There is a vast amount of literature on Gandhi, both biographical and fictional, I have restricted myself to two contemporary dramatic versions.
7. I have seen only one performance directed by Bhanu Bharati staged in Jaipur which was a one-actor presence on the stage with no technological interventions. Somehow, it failed to come alive. Its fidelity to the text subtracted from it rather than enhance or dramatize the conflict.

8. This was a very popular song which, once it became popular, Williams was asked to sing wherever he went. The first stanza runs like this and the last line is a refrain:

   When life seems full of clouds and rain/And I am filled with naught but pain/, Who soothes my thumping, bumping brain?/[pause] Nobody.
9. Refer *Autobiography*, pp. 220–222. Also see Rustom Bharucha's *Rajasthan: An Oral History: Conversations with Komal Kothari* (New Delhi: Penguin, 2003). Ong's work includes memorization, chanting and sound as ways of continuing oral traditions (see Ong. 57–65).

REFERENCES

Acharya, Nand Kishore. *Bapu* (Hindi). Unpublished manuscript. 2005.

"Bert Williams" internet source http://en.wikipedia.org/? title = Bert_Williams

Espinet, Ramabai. *Swinging Bridge*, New Delhi: Penguin, 2003.

Gandhi, M.K. *An Autobiography: The Story of My Experiments with Truth* (1927). Ahmedabad: Navjivan Mudranalaya, 1997.

Goffman, Erving. *The Presentation of Self in Everyday Life*, New York: Doubleday Anchor Books, 1959.

Kakar, Sudhir. *Intimate Relations: Exploring Indian Sexuality*. 1989. New Delhi: Penguin, 1990.

Man, Paul de "'Autobiography' as De-facement", *Deconstruction: A Reader*. Ed. Martin McQuillan. Edinburgh: Edinburgh University Press, 2000.

Ong, Walter J. *Orality and Literacy* (1982) London: Routledge, 2002.

Phillips, Caryl. *Dancing in the Dark* (2005). London: Vintage, 2006.

Sharma, Partap. *Sammy! The Word That Broke an Empire*. Mumbai: Rupa & Co. in association with Gandhi Smarak Nidhi. 2005.

CHAPTER 8

Becoming Canadian, Becoming Indian

History, Politics and Ideology in *Maluka*

Harish Narang

In a seminar held in Delhi on Sajaad Zaheer, a well-known Urdu author, renowned writers of stories in Hindi and novelist, Kamleshwar observed that the first book of a writer is generally based on his or her own self. He was referring to Sajaad Zaheer's novella—*London ki Ek Raat*. Now, it is a commonplace that most writers milk their own lives for filling the pages of most of their books. If this be so, I wondered, as to why Kamleshwar chose to state the obvious. But then I also recalled the context, namely, that *London ki Ek Raat* can be categorized as diasporic writing, since it was written during Sajaad Zaheer's long stay abroad when he was studying in London.

Diasporic writing, like most other writing, is about the self—only more pronounced. It is more pronounced because most diasporic writers draw their primary sustenance of 'lived experience' from not one but two societies—the donor and the host. They become children of two cultures.

A number of diasporic authors write not only their selves into their writings but also their communities. The most obvious names that come to one's mind are M.G. Vassanji whose novels and stories revolve around the Ismaili community whom he fictionalizes under the name of Shamsis and Rohinton Mistry who writes about the Parsi community to which he belongs.

Writing about one's self and at the same time writing about one's community from a diasporic location involves questions of identity—historical and cultural. In fact, the significance of most diasporic writing lies in the in-between space of hybrid identity that diasporic persons and communities come to acquire. Let me, therefore, recall, first of all, the manner in which identities—individual, communal and national—are formed and how these come to be mutated in situations where people have moved from one national location to another for various reasons.

Identity formation, we know, is a very complex phenomenon. It is a mixed bag of various markers or tokens—some are allotted at birth, some bestowed by the surrounding environment and some others obtained by being member of a particular community—within the bounds of a nation or without—and still some others earned through individual efforts. Thus dark skins and closely knit curly hair are the identity markers of those who belong to most nations of Africa, while pale skins, small eyes with slanted eyebrows and short frames of body are the tokens of identity of those belonging to nations in the Far East. These tokens are racial and ethnic in nature and are most stable of markers since they are difficult to change or shed either individually or communally, although a facial surgery carried out successfully in France a couple of months ago only shows that such identity markers for individuals may become unstable very soon and it may become difficult to justify the shooting of an innocent person by merely stating that he/she was 'Asian looking' as was the case with a Latin American in the wake of 7/7 bombings in London.

These tokens of identity are, at times, associated with certain socio-cultural traits assigned to individuals belonging to certain communities or class of people. These are generally unfounded, negative in nature and help stereotype the 'other' in relation to the self. However, once the relationship between the token and a community trait has been established, it is very difficult to change or eliminate the perception or the accompanying prejudice. The most obvious example from the past with most disastrous consequences for humanity is that of associating darker skinned Africans with 'natural' inferiority of mind. The entire *raison d'etre* of colonization of Africa was built on these tokens of identity begotten at birth and their societal perception and prejudice by Europeans. Another example with obvious sexual overtones is that of fair-skinned, golden-haired European women—blondes—being dubbed as 'dumb'. So widespread is this stereotype that it has spawned a whole industry of what are called 'dumb blonde jokes' spread over hundreds of internet sites. It may be interesting to note in the context that no such prejudice exists against blonde men. However, it must be noted that such prejudicial perception also posits the opposite. For instance, persons of European descent—fair-skinned as they are—are posited as 'naturally' superior to those with not so fair skin. Such stereotyping is more pronounced in situations of diaspora, and hence is used frequently in diasporic writing to highlight the clash between socio-politico-cultural identities.

Some other markers of identity are bestowed by environment on members of a particular community. *Innuits*, for instance, unlike their other fellow Canadians, can reportedly divide the phenomenon of snow into at least six distinct categories primarily because snow is what they have all around them—all the time. My mother once told me of a community of *khojis*—cattle search specialists in the rural Panjab of her childhood that is now part of Pakistan—who could trace stolen cattle hundreds of miles away from the scene of the crime and beyond canals and similar water bodies by following the foot-marks of the cattle. And this, my mother added, in her engaging manner of narration, despite the thieves mixing the stolen cattle in their own large herds. This they could achieve because they were a community of cattle breeders themselves and had learned to distinguish each individual cattle by its pug-signature.

Though stable, these environment-given identity markers to members of specific communities have in most cases lost their relevance with changing patterns and pace of life. However, such markers do bestow certain qualities in abstraction—sharpness of observation, for instance—that in turn becoming the distinguishing feature of those communities as well as of their individual members. The *Marwari* community, for example, originated in the desert region of Rajasthan that was not only a land of deficiency but also where the means of transportation and communication were quite scarce. As a result, the community learnt to save and build reserves from really meagre resources. *Marwari* diaspora, now spread all over the world, is renowned today for building huge business empires out of very small beginnings, thanks to this environmentally dictated trait of theirs.

Most numerous and most significant, however, are the identity markers that are cultural in character. These involve language and religious beliefs, customs and habits, forms of address and modes of interpersonal behaviour, dress codes and food habits, form and content of education, songs and stories, symbols and icons, myths and legends, practices for preserving history and tradition and many other similar things. Add to these, modes of production, economic, political and societal organization, professional and philosophical preferences and we have the complete cultural cartography of communities and individuals. Most writing—either highlighting the self or community or even nation, diasporic or otherwise—uses this as a basic raw material. However, despite being most numerous, these identity markers are relatively more unstable.

In a typical diaspora situation, that is, when members of a community from a nation go away—the factors necessitating this could be either 'pull' or 'push' or both, the reasons could range from political persecution to highly paid jobs in reputed multinationals—one of the first adjustments that the newly arrived have to make is to acquire new identities, almost immediately, although they are still carrying their old ones on their persons and more significantly in their minds. Thus they become hybrids when they give up some of the original cultural identity markers and acquire corresponding markers from the mainstream of the society they are migrating into. These denote, in a way, the cultural visa stamp for entry into the society. Some of these tokens, the immigrants are ready to shed easily and without much fuss, while there are some others they give up only reluctantly, and there are still some more that they want to keep as long as they can.

The tokens from the first and the third categories mentioned above, namely, those begotten at birth and those acquired culturally are the ones that provide sites for contestation and consequential conflict between the host and donor societies. Most negative stereotypes are built around these. For instance, for many Europeans, in terms of a biological identity marker, white pigmentation still signifies purity, knowledge and overall superiority of mind, whereas black stands for ignorance, evil, primitiveness and is the cause of many a conflict and discrimination in societies where Africans are in diasporic situation. The criminal official neglect of people of African American community in New Orleans in the USA during the devastation caused by hurricane Catarina is attributed to such a prejudice. Again, religious belief systems of diasporic people are at times considered inferior and subjected to ridicule as well as discrimination. The current controversy around the cartoons involving Prophet Mohammed in a Danish newspaper is one such example arising out of the European prejudice that most followers of Islam are terrorists. The early Indian immigrants to Canada, for instance, were run down for being polygamists in a country that was by religious belief a monogamist society. In France, not allowing school girls from Islamic background to wear *hijab* or not allowing Sikh boys to wear little symbolic *kirpans* on their bodies, while placing no such restrictions on the wearing of the 'cross' are recent examples of identity markers spawning conflict in situations that Edward Said termed as 'crossing over'.

There are, however, certain tokens of identity that people in diasporic situations shed readily and easily. The dress code for instance. In the next part of this presentation I shall have the opportunity to show how the early immigrants to Canada willingly dressed themselves in European clothes even while waiting to board the ships at Hong Kong. The speed and readiness with which immigrant Indian women—even those belonging to conservative, middle-class families—shed their *sarees* and *salwar-kameez* to don European dresses or stop using *bindi* and *sindoor*—identity markers of married status of many women—are all signs of the same desire to assimilate. Not only dress but language too is an easy prey to such 'identitarian' politics, to borrow another expression from Said. The promptness with which the Gujarati *dukawallas* in East Africa picked up 'Jambo' and 'Karibu Sana' or the efforts put into by even highly educated and professional Indian immigrants to the USA in learning the American 'accent' highlight the same desire to homogenize *suo motto*.

There are, however a large number of cultural tokens that the diaspora people are most unwilling to give up even under intense social, economic and political pressures. Early Sikh immigrants, as stated above, were willing to dress themselves up in European dresses but were not willing to part with their *pagris*—the headgear—ordained by their religion. For Muslim migrants to eat non-*halal* meat or pork products, and for Hindu immigrants to consume beef are examples of similar cultural tokens that stand in the way of integration and are at times resented by host societies.

And now let me explicate briefly on the diasporic writers. Writers of the diaspora are different from others in the sense that they operate from this twilight zone—we may call it the diasporic experience—to which they themselves belong as individuals and as members of a community or a nation. The diasporic experience may be likened to riding two horses simultaneously. And if this is not adventurous enough, the two horses—representing the two cultures of the donor and the recipient societies—are pulling the individual into two different directions. While the host or the recipient national society eggs the individual on to move ahead full steam and integrate and assimilate with the mainstream, the donor society may be trying to hold him or her back, to retain the individual as a part of its cultural community as far as and as long as possible.

The tension generated by this simultaneous pulling in two different—if not diametrically opposite—directions is what diasporic writers relish. In terms of our earlier proposition of identity markers this tension consists of dealing in a new mixed currency comprising some old tokens that are retained because they cannot be shed, at least not easily, and some others are given up—voluntarily, and at times not so voluntarily— are replaced by new ones acquired as a part of the process of integration and assimilation. As observed above, diasporic writers relish this in-between space—the discomfiture on the part of the diasporic community in riding two horses simultaneously or their awkwardness in handling a mix of new and old currency of identity tokens—because creativity lies in portraying this difficult choice between 'to be' or 'not to be'.

Since this in-between world of the diasporic experience is inhabited by individuals as members of a particular community or a nation, writers of diaspora while writing individual's self, in most cases—also write communities and nations from locations that may be termed as 'beyond' or, as I once called them 'nations beyond nations'. And since diasporic communities bring in their gunny sacks—physical and cerebral—their histories and politics, their pride and prejudice—I almost said brides and prejudice—writers of diaspora bring in—almost invariably, almost inevitably—references to the history of such communities. Thus in writing the self of other individuals in diasporic situations, these writers are writing simultaneously communities and their pasts. As mentioned above, the two whose names spring to one's mind most immediately are M.G. Vassanji and Rohinton Mistry. Vassanji writes of Shamsi individuals, the Shamsi community and its origin back in India, while Mistry focuses his fictional gaze on the Parsi community in India to which he himself belongs. Other writers like Uma Parameswaran, Lakshmi Gill, Cyril Dabydeen, Nalini Warrior, Hiro Boga, Rana Bose, Sadhu Binning, Suniti Namjoshi, Ramabai Espinet and Surjeet Kalsey all invoke their communities and their respective pasts in their poems, plays and stories in order to highlight their predicament of being and becoming. There is one who, however, is lesser known but whose only book *Maluka* fictionalizes the story of those early immigrants in a very different manner and with a different world view.

S.S. Dhami's *Maluka,* the first part of which was published in 1978 and the second, nine years later in 1989, is a novel that has all the three features of diasporic writing, namely, self, community and history. *Maluka,* in more than one ways, is Dhami's own story. It is the story of his arrival in Canada at a tender age—his very name, Maluka, means 'tender' in his mother tongue Punjabi—after dropping out of school back in India, earning his living as a lumberjack in various parts of Vancouver in British Columbia on the west coast, and working his way up through education to a doctoral degree from the University of Toronto, and then ending up as a respectable official with the ILO, first in Canada and later in Geneva. Simultaneously, *Maluka* is the story of the formation of the Indian diaspora in Canada when the first batches of pioneer Sikhs arrived on the Pacific coast to work on lumber mills, railroad projects and jungle-clearing operations. At the level of history, Dhami brings alive the extraordinary times—the British Empire, Indian Freedom Struggle, the Ghadar Party, the Great Depression and the World War I, and Canada's engagement with all these while grappling with problems of its own being and becoming as a nation with a distinct identity. We shall see how Dhami works out these various strands to weave, to borrow a phrase from M.G. Vassanji, 'a living tapestry' of Indian diaspora in Canada.

At one level—the most obvious one—*Maluka* is the story of a school-lad from rural Punjab who gave up school and arrived in Canada at a tender age to work along with grown up, mostly middle-aged Sikhs, who as individuals were engaged in earning a living in appalling working conditions in the lumber mills and railroad related projects around Vancouver region in British Columbia:

> Here in the New World, so clean and prosperous, the Punjabi workers went about, except on week-ends, in messy blue working clothes, like the coolies, and lived like the Chinese, in slummy little ghettoes in Vancouver, or in ramshackle shed on the work premises, isolated from the local people who looked down upon them. At the Dominion Mills they lived in bunk houses. Six long parallel sheds with tarred paper roofs, each partitioned into small rooms with two bunks in each. They had been built on the marshy bank of the Fraser filled with the mill refuse and covered over by soggy layers of sawdust. With time, they had acquired a weather-beaten dark gray look, and had sunk almost foot into the sawdust. In the passage way of these sheds, on both sides, hung dirty working clothes, almost touching the rows of heavy working shoes and the black gum boots under them, and on the work-out boards of the floor the nail heads stood bare and shiny. (9)

To young Maluka, this was so very different from 'the leisurely old world' he had left behind:

> the blooming fields of cotton and corn, the dark-green groves of mango trees, the long-horned cattle with beautiful humps, and the creaking wooden carts moving so as not to blow the dust ... Men and women in flowing colourful garments walking and talking noisily in the crowded bazaar; the shoppers resting under the shady trees by the roadside sharing titbits and gossip. Young girls with twinkling black eyes and gleaming white teeth spinning at their hand wheels and singing; boisterous boys with lithe brown bodies playing *kabadi* in the moonlight; happy families gathered around the hearth in the dim light for a simple meal. Pictures so bright and gay so vivid and yet so far. (2)

But at another level, it is not the story of Maluka alone but of the entire community of immigrants from India who were laying the first bricks of what was to become a magnificent edifice of Indian diaspora in Canada—a community that was trying deliberately to grow out of their past and look forward to the future. As Natha Singh, a former non-commissioned officer of the British Army in India and now a fellow worker in Dominion Mills, puts it to Maluka whom he is trying to educate:

> 'You are young, Maluka,' he said with an avuncular concern. 'And youth is like the river. It always looks ahead.' 'But the river has no memories', replied Maluka pensively. 'It has memories, Maluka,' said Natha Singh with emphasis, 'but it doesn't brood over them. It carries them in its quiet flow. But it cannot go back to the mountains no matter how sharp and fresh the memories. It sings its way to the sea.' Maluka got up with a lump in his throat. 'Look at me', continued Natha Singh as he patted him on the back. 'I am getting old but I still look ahead. Like every one, I carry my past within me, and at times its burden feels heavy. But I don't brood over it.' (3)

However, the future too does not hold much promise for these pioneer Sikhs who become victims of their most stable identity marker—their ethnicity, their non-European origin. Again, 'I' is Natha Singh, who draws Maluka's attention to the discrimination against them:

> 'Several of us who have worked on the green chain for eight or ten years know enough about lumber to do the grading better than Guss', added Natha Singh after straightening the pieces on the truck with quick flips by his hands. 'But none of us, nor any other oriental, no matter how good, would be employed as a grader or a tally man in the lumberyard.'

To me the most crucial word in that observation by Natha Singh is 'oriental'. By using that word instead of 'Indian', Natha Singh is setting up a unity that goes beyond the narrow national community bonds in fighting prejudice. That this crucial lesson in the education of Maluka is not lost on him is evident from his subsequent concern for all workers—white or non-white, Indian or Chinese.

In fact, the perspective stays with him through his movement upwards and when he finally accepts a job, it is only in the field of work close to his heart. The novel ends with Maluka accepting to work with the ILO, an organization that is concerned with 'improvement of labour conditions in the world' (344).

Again, these simple, rustic unlettered people from Punjab refused to fall in the most obvious trap of *us* versus *them*, the so-called inherent contradictions of host and donor societies and cultures:

> They told of the kindness of many Canadians, in particular, the women who gave them warm clothings when they landed in the cold winter ...

But then Maluka and his mentors at the Dominion Mills—Natha Singh and Ganda Singh and Tara Singh and many more Singhs—were as much progressive and forward-looking when it came to thinking about the community and the country they had left behind. Coming to Canada as the loyal subjects of the British Empire they were intrigued by the refusal of the Canadian government to let the passengers of Komagatamaru to set foot on His Majesty's soil, although many of them had 'served the Crown', they soon learned to look at things holistically and discovered the sinister links between the discrimination against them in Canada and their colonized status back home:

> The proud Punjabis in the New World, unable to secure redress for the discrimination they suffered, asked themselves a simple question. What right can a people expect to enjoy in a foreign country when they had none in their own ? So long as India remained subjugated, they concluded, they would continue to be treated as collies abroad. To free India, therefore, was the basic problem. It was the first task to be undertaken. But how is power to be dislodged? By force, of course. Long ago, Maharaja Ranjit Singh had replied to the Englishman who wanted to know the price of the Kohinoor: 'I got it by the sword; you will get it the same way.' (27)

The treatment meted out to the passengers of Komagatamaru only reinforced their resolve and, as Banta Singh puts it to Maluka, their loyalty to the British 'slipped' with the slipping away of the ship from Canadian waters.

Here too Dhami would steer clear of ethnic divide, making it a more political divide on the basis of class. It is a Socialist white Canadian, Fitzgerald, who waged while addressing the

Sunday congregation of Punjabis, to 'sweep all the whites from India' (25).

The place where all these discussions took place, where the observations were made was called 'cookhouse'. Designed as a long shed, lying perpendicularly to bunk houses with a huge cooking stove in one corner and an old oblong heater in the centre and long table covered with oil cloth and wooden benches by them on three sides, the cookhouse was an amazing space, a Trafalgar Square of sorts, a diasporic people's parliament where 'reading aloud of newspapers was a popular and a more regular source of entertainment', and where the literate reader enjoyed an enviable status, where quick comments and pointed questions often led to a lively discussion and at times to a heated argument. It is in the cookhouse that it was debated whether Gandhi—that rabbit-eared Bania from Gujarat, as Ganda Singh described him—was a villain or a hero of the Indian freedom struggle, where a non-believer like Ganda Singh, a communist, was likened to 'a son without a father' by a religious zealot like Bhai Tara Singh, who, Ganda alleged in return, wrote to Amritsar to ask whether to eat in a non-*jhatka* restaurant in Vancouver. And all this take place without rancour or raising of their voices. It is here that they discuss the prejudice of the white Miss Catherine Maynard against them who observed that 'the Hindus have horrible social customs. They marry their girls too young, for they prefer to eat their fruit raw. They produce little food, but many children. Early and excessive sex leaves them impotent at twenty-nine.' And the retort from Jagga the Jack that he 'didn't even see a pair of naked legs till afer twenty-nine.'

The cookhouse is created by Dhami as the site where a contestation takes place with a polyphony of voices in the true Bakhtinian sense. And for Maluka, the cookhouse was his first school where he:

> soon learned a great deal about the life and the problems of these simple outspoken villagers from the Punjab, who had left their homes for a distant land to secure a better living. The difficulties they had faced in the New World, together with the racial discrimination,

resented more than anything else by these proud people, had made them stick together in small communities for companionship and warmth of feeling, which they needed to live the customary open-hearted village life sharing much with each other' (21).

It is here that the 'proud Punjabis in the New World, unable to secure redress for the discrimination they suffered, asked themselves a simple question, What right can a people expect to enjoy in a foreign country when they had none in their own? So long as India remained subjugated, they concluded, they would continue to be treated as coolies abroad. To free India, therefore, was the basic problem. It was the first task to be undertaken' (27).

Urging young Maluka not to 'get stuck in a lumber mill like us', they asked him to 'study and learn to write' and write their story with his blood 'hot and boiling'.

The rest of the novel is a long and winding narrative—with the *leitmotif* of quest for self—of the trials and tribulations of Maluka in fulfilling these twin tasks—of educating himself and telling their story—that the founding fathers of Indian diasporic society in Canada bestowed on him. While characterizing the foundations of Canada as exploitative of the diasporic communities, Maluka did not lose any opportunity to reiterate his empathy for all those on the margins irrespective of their ethnicity or nationality. That is how he abstracted the lessons he learnt from 'the older men' who 'loved to tell stories about their early experiences in British Columbia'. Some of them, as Dhami observes, 'had the rare gift of the oriental story-teller' (23).

So the river was indeed trying to go back to the mountain—to gain a fresh and more vigorous mandate for moving forward. Sitting thousands of miles away, sipping hot tea that was available on tap, they were discussing and debating their lives in Canada, analysing their predicament to link it with that of fellow Indians back home. And they did not just fume and fret. To begin with, they supported the Ghadr movement—collected money for its cause, published newspapers, organized and addressed gatherings, admired and respected its leaders: Jawala Singh, Sohan Sing Bhakna, Kartar Singh Sarabha and Barkatullah and many others. Simultaneously, they learned about and linked their fate with white Canadians in similar situations of exploitation—and there were many—and the struggling masses elsewhere. If they did not do one thing, it was to give in to despair.

And Maluka, a fast learner, soon felt the need for resuming his formal education that he had given up in India on the call of Mahatma Gandhi. To build on what he had learnt of Gandhi's call of non-cooperation and later in the cookhouse, he moved to a high school in the Fraser area—John Oliver High School was its name—and then on to the university of Alberta and finally to the Universities of Toronto and California. However, it was to the cookhouse that he continued to return even after the Dominion Mill had been burnt in an accident and its residents scattered, with the same sense of reverence and in the same spirit with which scholars return to their alma maters. As he tells Anna, his friend who had come to Canada as a Jewish German refugee during the war as to why had he suddenly decided to go to British Columbia at the height of his career in Toronto in 1938:

> '... The small Punjabi community there was my second home and my first university. I grew very fond of it ... . Strong, simple men from the countryside ... they faced life with amazing courage and great joy. Most of them were illiterate, and yet they encouraged me to study ... . I can still hear their voices: Study, Maluka, Study. Don't end up like us—sawdust on our turbans and sawdust in our heads. You must study Maluka, and write our story' (323).

To cut the presentation short, *Maluka* is very different from other diasporic discourses about Indo-Canadians of the early years. It brings out very poignantly, very vividly and very significantly the story of the pioneer Punjabis in Canada who suffered all kinds of hardships and discriminations but who did not surrender their self-respect; nor did they fall victims to racial prejudice in reverse and surrender their humanity. In their process of becoming more Canadians, they also became more

Indians. In the post-9/11 and post-7/7 world where the future of non-white diasporic communities in Europe and North America is once again in the balance, where people are being killed by the state terror for being 'Asian looking' or sporting long beards or having Islamic-looking names, the significance of Dhami's message of inclusion rather than exclusion needs to be invoked afresh—both by the donor and host nation societies. We need to rise above narrow national negativities. The million dollar question is, will we?

REFERENCE

Dhami, S.S., *Maluka*, New Delhi, Arnold Heinemann, 1978, 1989.

CHAPTER 9

Beyond Purdah

Intersubjectivity and Interstitiality in Imtiaz Dharker's Poetry

Sudha Rai

The contemporary is a stage fraught with the contestations of multiple agencies of nation, media and religion, vying to construct and manipulate identities, often conformist and fundamentalist in character. In this scenario, poets continue to raise their non-fragmented secular voices to sensitize readers to their need to reclaim their own selves, in quiet sanctuaries, the 'interstitial' spaces of deeply awakened consciousness of the self, countering nationalist rhetoric and other discourses of power.

A unique contemporary poetic voice, forging a synergy of image, text and poetic voice, that compels the reader to a stern confrontation of the polarization of religious and national identities, is that of the diasporic poet Imtiaz Dharker. A Pakistani-British poet brought up in Glasgow, Dharker brings to her artistic perspective experiences of her gendered Muslim identity, multiracial British ethnicity, and socio-political realities of post-1990s India. As poet, artist and documentary film maker, Dharker exposes the ideological strategies for production of packaged identities by various political and religious groups.

The self-reflective journey of a constantly expanding intersubjectivity, a journey carried out through the 'third spaces' of an interstitially positioned self in Dharker's poetry, enables a theorization of the concepts of 'identity', 'subjectivity' and 'intersubjectivity' related to the discovery of the 'self.' The poetic process that plots this journey of differences, diversities and pluralities will be illustrated in the present paper from Dharker's four anthologies of poetry.

As a *genre* endowed with a potential for philosophical penetration, Dharker's poetry approaches the specific political realities of modern national histories of Partition or communalism, through the poetic currency of suggestive political allegories, provoking the reader to question universally relevant situations of authority and subjugation. Working her way through obliquely rendered critiques, Dharker evokes the lurking 'terror' of identity appropriation, so destructive to the freedom of the self and the ideal goal of intersubjective existence in her terms.

Poetry, a marginalized *genre*, with its disruptive linguistic constructions and rhythms, is perhaps a more suitable channel for unmasking political rhetoric, fixed community and religious identities, and for piercing the walled silences of the marginalized. The poetic voice can work as a scalpel to pare away the density of power-strata and social discourses that do continue to produce subjugated and conforming identities.

Working against the grain of existing full-blown master narratives of women's and communal identity, choosing the poetic voice against the more solid currency of prose, Dharker's poetic images, and juxtaposed drawings, pierce intellectual obfuscations, stirring our submerged conscience, our instinct for humanity, the awareness of injustice, the need for joy and dignity. Endorsing that the 'small is beautiful' and the realm of in-between is truthful, the poems educate the reader on the necessity of linking the persona's own humane subjectivity with the subjectivity of neglected persons, places, and artifacts. In this way her recent poems in *The Terrorist at my Table* break out of the limiting frame of centre and periphery of Muslim identity. Dharker began her journey with the *Purdah*, opening up to states of evolutionary consciousness that drew sustenance from the 'interstitial' of the postcolonial theorist Homi Bhabha, or the 'intersubjective' being debated in philosophy.

II

A number of critical positions arising from postcolonial, feminist, gender and postmodernist debates converge on the notion of the 'self' and its formation. Though at variance with the processes of formation of the self and the hierarchy they occupy, the three related concepts of identity, subjectivity and intersubjectivity (that my paper correlates) have been theorized significantly from within the domains of psychology and philosophy and literature, (though the debates have been raised in politics and sociology as well). The debates look closely at the construction of the individual 'I' of identity/subjectivity, examining the positive or obstructive role, as the case may be of cultural and historical forces in their formation. Can the individual identity (derived from a group and national identity) free itself of the trap of essentialism? Is subjectivity as much as identity, a necessary stage of ego formation, that must be transcended? Is intersubjectivity a higher state, a state of trans-identity, a desired evolutionary stage of the self?

While the initial location of Dharker in her first anthology, *Purdah*, is within the binary of centre and periphery of Muslim religion—the leaders and the women in Purdah, her collection *The Terrorist at my Table*, explores events and phenomena by turning the narrative eye on the flow of persona and consciousness that, crossing various borders (literal and metaphoric) counter the imprisoning identities of the contemporary. The dialogic relationship that Dharker initiates is between one interstitial cultural space and another, sites for illumination of the truth.

In his study of cultural identity of Indians, Sudhir Kakar suggests: 'Identity is not a role, or a succession of roles, with which it is often confused. It is not a garment that can be put on or taken off according to the weather outside; it is not "fluid", but marked by a sense of continuity and sameness irrespective of where the person finds himself during the course of his life. A man's identity—of which the culture that he has grown up in is a vital part—is what makes him recognize himself and *be recognized* by the people who constitute his world. It is not something he has chosen, but something that has seized him. It can hurt, be cursed or bemoaned but cannot be discarded, though it can always be concealed from others or, more tragic, from one's own self' (Kakar and Kakar, 2).

Subjectivity is a term that is sometimes dealt with separately from the concept of identity and sometimes has overlapping connotations. It stresses 'personal feelings and experience,' 'self-knowing autonomous identity' and 'occurs in conjunction with such concepts as identity, the self, the individual, and the human being' (Harting, 2005).

Harting observes:

> ... contemporary concepts of subjectivity emphasize the link between power, language, and identity and the fundamental interdependence of human beings with their environment. It is by being part of a highly interconnected and violent world that human beings articulate, who they think they are in terms of complex networks of sexual, racial, ethnic, familial, colonial, political, institutional, and cultural identifications. In recent years, humanist and psychoanalytical concepts of subjectivity have given way to post-colonial and feminist understandings of the concept ... that have "generated new subjectivities."

While identities of race, gender and class are determined by cultural and historical formations as we now know, an awareness regarding the fixed boundaries of identity in the modern age has led to the privileging of subjectivity as an authentic formation of self, an 'experienced interiority'.

Intersubjectivity, again, has been defined in different ways: 'Through intersubjectivity one thus experiences oneself as different from the Other and at the same time available to him. This is a key component in the constitution of one's own existence as objectively existing subjectivity' (Wikepedia).

By and large, the term emphasizes that shared cognition, and consensus is essential in the shaping of our ideas and relations. While from one perspective intersubjectivity is seen as the binding thread of cultural and communitarian, identity and its language, with possible negative connotations of fixity and closure, other positions point to a positive potential within intersubjectivity for the expansion and connection of selves across boundaries.

Is intersubjectivity then a form of trans-identity, both transcendent and transformative? How can intersubjectivity dissolve narrow identities and connect subjectivities? Dharker's poems in *The Terrorist at my Table* set up woman-to-woman intersubjectivities established through both gendered and de-gendered linkages, and the diasporic bridges of her own journey that encourage an expansive movement of selfhood. Harting (2005) draws attention to Julia Kristeva's 'linguistic and intersubjective model of subjectivity,' 'a maternally defined pre-symbolic space that destabilizes and intrudes into the symbolic space of patriarchal representation and subject formation.'

The construction of intersubjectivities is complicated within the global present by the factor of excessive mobility: Blommaert suggests that the mobility we have to understand is not mobility across empty spaces, but mobility across spaces filled with codes, customs, rules, expectations and so forth. 'Mobility is an itinerary across normative spaces, and these spaces are always somebody else's spaces' (Blommaert, 2005). Negotiating normativity through diasporic mobility, Dharker creates a pattern of perforated dots that the reader has to string into a set of significances and/or values.

The term 'interstitial' (Bhabha) seems to be a particularly appropriate one to characterize Dharker's diasporic condition of in-betweenness, referring to her cumulative cultural background formed in Lahore, Glasgow and Mumbai. Interstitiality also evokes her preference for the poetic mode over the novelistic and her subjective artistic location between drawing and poetry. Unique, within the South Asian diasporic literary context, her anthologies of poetry are an assemblage of incisive and evocative line drawings that are in dialogue with the poems on the printed page, creating echoes and ripples between visual art, and human language.

Within the domain of architecture, 'an interstitial space is a small or narrow area that occurs between other things and is generally overlooked and undesigned.' In the visual arts, 'interstitial art is a term first coined in the 1990s, and increasingly popularized in the early 2000s, that refers to any work of art whose basic nature falls between, rather than within, the familiar boundaries of accepted genres or media, thus making the work difficult to easily categorize or describe within a single artistic discipline' (Wikepedia).

Whether the condition of hybridity needs to be held, without erasing the hyphen as Uma Parameswaran believes, or a diasporic fluid identity is more valuable, has generated debates, relating to the contexts of dispersal, national and transnational affiliation. Gayatri Spivak feels that for her, 'the question "Who should speak?" is less crucial than "Who will listen" '(59). Issues of agency, audience, context of hegemonic communities, the real other and re-formation of new subjectivities determine the efficacy of the diasporic third space.

Humanistic discourse itself can be misleading. Bruce Robbins (Ray, 562) states: 'In sum, the real issue is not humanism and universalism, neither of which can be identified with a single geographically defined set of interests or simply opposed in the abstract. The issue is what particular content has been throwing its weight under cover of positions either for or against these large abstractions.' Dharker's dissenting poetic voices, women-centric outsiders, rise to a crescendo in exposing the reality behind the fundamentalist discourses of humanism.

III

'Purdah', in the poems of Dharker's volume by that name, both reality and metaphor, captures the claustrophobic fear and the objectification of Muslim women confined behind the veil, denied the powers of rational and imaginative agency. The poems point to a women's legacy of shame, sin, dislocation from their natural selves, alienated by their hostage positions within the scrutiny of the male gaze and its voyeurism. In 'Purdah I', 'the veil becomes "a cloth" that fans out against the skin/much like the earth that falls/on coffins after they put the dead men in.' All exits being barred, Dharker touches the despair of an existence where 'doors keep opening/inward and again/inward.'

In the interrogation of the unsafe religious spaces of a governing patriarchy, Dharker focuses on the vulnerable female body, a target for indoctrination. The abuse of women as commodities within marriage, is summed up in the candid generalization: 'They have all been sold and bought,/the girls I knew ...' The misleading bond of the intersubjectivity of Muslim women's identity, founded in a fixed religious identity is questioned by Dharker: 'The body, rocked in time/With twenty others, was lulled/Into thinking it had found a home' (Purdah: 5).

That this Purdah identity, a historical and social construction is normative, manifests, when Naseem dares to transgress the traditional norms for marriage, by having a relationship with an English boy and is disowned summarily by mothers and aunts alike: 'The table is laden at Moharram/And you are remembered among the dead. No going back. The prayers said.'

The uncharted journey of the self, that 'one coin, one sound' of freedom, is the undestroyed pathway of discovery of the self celebrated by the persona. In the poem 'Grace,' the counter discourse against the appropriation of a woman's self by the patriarchal irrational, brings about an awakening within the female consciousness: 'He rolls his reason on his tongue And spits it out; You know again the drought/The blazing eye of faith can bring about' (Purdah: II).

From where does Imtiaz Dharker speak? In *Purdah*, the debates are generated in an oppositional space, where the gendered Muslim subject interrogates the closures of patriarchal Muslim religion. In her second anthology *Postcards from God*, Dharker creates a new mythical space for Godhead, delinked from any specific religion. The voice of a disillusioned God, spectator to orgies of violence (of which the 1992 Bombay terrorist attacks were an example), is a satirical voice, expounds the need for a morality of the commonality of humans over their difference: Things were meant to flow one from another they were meant to grow into one another; to know the taste and feel of being part of one vast whole (Words Find Mouths: 21).

The moralistic, doomsday tone of the persona, consciously steers the reader to take stock of an eroded centre of ethics. The imaginary Godhead confesses a virtual powerlessness to deal with human insanity. The collection of poems in *Postcard* is a creative rejoinder to the fallout of religion in the shape of fundamentalism especially in the 1990s (in India and globally), suggesting God's need to communicate his original vision of humanity, through communications on the humble postcard, not on canonized tomes.

Dharker endows God with a new dialogic identity, responsive to human interrogation. In the poem 'Monsters Grow Out of My Image,' the separation between spirituality (God) and the contemporary human is summed up in judgmental terms: 'Everywhere you scream my words,/but you forget my name'.

Censorship of the individual's speech is a reality that Dharker asks us to reflect on in religious, gender and national contexts. Perhaps this is the reason why her third and fourth anthologies of poetry—*I Speak For the Devil* and *The Terrorist at My Table* are more 'talkative texts,' their voices of resistance, making a departure from the silences and the interior stream of consciousness monologues and dialogues in the poems in *Purdah*.

A repudiation of the patriarchal construction of women, the poems in *I Speak for the Devil* such as 'Honour Killing' shows us a woman persona denuding/peeling her entire body and being, so as to begin afresh, discarding identity and initiating a new subjectivity:

I'm taking off this skin and then the face, the flesh, the womb. Let's see what I am in here, making, crafting, plotting at my new geography. (5)

The diasporic inter-subjectivity of multiple identities and allegiances is upheld, against the normative expectation to live in and fulfil any single national identity: And so my mouth spoke Punjabi while my brain heard Scots. My ears followed German and my tongue did French. It seemed they were about to put me out in a garbage bag, I looked so odd. But I survived (11).

Spatial metaphors of 'Here' and 'There': Journeys, arrivals and departures mark the process of dismantling of the given—'Every new city, every street/I get to pull the ground away/from underneath my feet' (12). The persona in 'Front Door' is '... high on the rush of daily displacement ...' (18).

Working their way through disparate geographies and languages, Dharker's personas reach out to the reader extending a helping hand, enabling a journey of intersubjectivity as in the lines from the poem 'Front Door'—'Don't think I haven't noticed you're on the same trip too' (18).

In Dharker's 'Not a Muslim burial,' we witness a radical overthrow of the persona's Muslim identity: 'No one must claim me./On the journey I will need/no name, no nationality./Let them label the remains/Lost Property' (29).

A poem of angry protest and stark exposure of power structures, the passionate defence of the interstitial location is presented in 'They'll say, "She must be from another country" ': 'May be there is a country where all of us live, all of us freaks who aren't able to give our loyalty to fat old fools the crooks and thugs who wear the uniform.'

Through reimagined spatial metaphors, the persona envisions another country: 'But from where we are it doesn't look like a country, its more like the cracks that grow between borders behind their backs. That's where I live ...' (31).

The poem beckon to readers to involve themselves in giving birth to a new self: 'You once had an idea/of yourself/kiss it goodbye' (93).

The 'devils' in the title of the collection stand for the misleading taboos and proscribed phenomena, and for women who desire a sensuous and rational apprehension of the world. The images of partially disrobed or naked women contest the ideological trap, as the women seek escape by their airborne journeys, from the clutches of the social demons.

Structured in three sections, Dharker's *The Terrorist at my Table,* searches for the spirit of place, in cities from Glasgow to Mumbai and Lahore, and in identities, whether Black, British, Muslim or diasporic in-between. The poems open up the feelings, fears, habits, dress, and desires of predominantly its women personae. Contemporary themes that are taken up in the anthology and expressed through metropolitan locations and experiences, and the identity politics of race and religion, bring before us the knowing consciousness of the persona aware of being caught in masquerades that threaten the sanctuary of freedom. The poems speak of the enemy within, the penetration of terror within our safe borders and sanctuaries, which are then placed beside the search for a resilient life and resistant spirit: 'A Cyclops in motion/A hulk on the screen he's seen every angle and been many things to many people and if he has a mind its his own' (126).

The sequence of poems takes up the life of 'the girl with red ribbons,' penetrating to her interior life of joy, despite her set and mechanical life—'from home to water/from water back to home' (129). In the sequence of poems 'Rickshaw Ride', Dharker's evolution in perspective becomes evident as each character—the girl, the rickshaw driver, the rickshaw rider, the media Mogul intersect in reality and history, showing different facets of their lives—not better or worse, but inclusive.

Dharker targets identities packaged by the strategies of media in this collection. Contemporary images of the proliferation of images generated by TV channel networks, are highlighted in 'Screen' and 'Ends of the Earth.' The poem plays on vocabulary generated from the root word 'screen'—such as 'smokescreen,' 'snowscreen,' 'sunscreen' and the repetition of 'screen' throwing light on typical stories picked up by the entertainment and news media, a common code language of unexamined intersubjectivity: 'Here I am, showing/you the tenth of ninety-nine channels.' The persona opts out of these packaged identities—'Screen./Cover this./Hide this./Let me pass./I don't want to see/this' (135). In 'End of the Earth,' the persona laments the loss of privacy—'Seven of we had doors, nothing would keep/the other out./The world is with us too much'.

The rickshaw becomes in the sequence, a magical vehicle, capable of crossing boundaries and countries, now in Mumbai, then in Glasgow, the factory connecting the subjectivity of a childhood past and the journeys in the present. 'Home' and 'homelessness' change places. 'No paradise, this, where lost/souls cry in mobile phones' (154) or 'These giant screens hoisted at screen corners, making noisy promises' (154). The last poem in the sequence 'Halfway' revisits each character in the previous poems, encountered in the auto route: 'Halfway home or halfway one we have grown accustomed now to travelling on the faultline of daily miracles' (158).

The channel of poetry is perhaps a befitting one for unmasking political rhetoric, the intersubjectivity of fixed community and religious identities, bringing down the entrenched wall of stereotypes that keep the people of the margins buried and invisible. The poetic voice works as a scalpel, paring away the density of social discourses that produce subjugated and conforming identities. Working against the grain of the structure and texture of prose, Dharker's images pierce obfuscations, stirring the submerged conscience, the instinct for humanity, the awareness of injustice, the need for joy and dignity. Poems in the collection that endorse the principle, 'small is beautiful', educate the reader on the necessity of discovering the self, linking it with the subjectivity of neglected persons, places, creatures, artifacts, thereby orchestrating the rich diversity of life. Intersubjectivity takes the shape of a dialogic relationship between traditional hierarchies or disjunctive realities.

Another poem that tenderly evokes the meeting point of women's ungendered subjectivities through the metaphor of pomegranate seeds is 'The Women'. The persona sets out to meet all the women, as many in number as pomegranate seeds—'And I am on my way to meet them,/just one more seed,/flung a little further than the rest' (71).

Dharker's emphasis is on creating her own images, undoubtedly part of her artist's self, but also included to subvert the media images that generally distort and manipulate reality. The sketches are juxtaposed with clear, whole phrases, or overwritten, blurred and partially visible lines, from the poem that faces it in the layout of the text.

This fusion of image and line comes through strongly in *Terrorist at My Table*, in the section 'These and the Times We Live In.' The collage of text and sketch creates a disturbance in the reader, forced to confront the small print of reports on violence as is 'These are the times we live in I' (44). Bold headlines create a focus such as 'Dramatic breakthrough makes for gripping television,' or 'In Terror.'

The veil of a woman in *Purdah* is constituted out of a collage of news from the print media. Other subversive directions to the reader to interpret reality are contained in directions on the collage sketch, for example, 'See through the writing' and 'Look through the image' (48). In her article 'Media in a Capitalist Culture,' Barbara Treat exhorts us to empower ourselves through self-imaging rather than surrender this power to the global media. She states: 'We need to support ourselves, our sisters and our brothers in recording our own history and creating images of ourselves and the world that we can share with each other. It is time to take action' (Jameson, 246).

In his essay 'Notes on Globalization, a Philosophical Issue' (Jameson, 1998), Frederic Jameson theorizes the assimilatory function of globalization: 'Here what begins to infuse our thinking of globalization is a picture of standardization on an unparalleled new scale; of forced integration as well, into a world system ...' (57). Dharker's thrust is to move beyond Identity and Difference, as binary counterparts, and arrive at a strategy of interconnectivity of phenomena as 'soul' rather than 'ego'.

Dharker's location as a 'minority,' as 'a foreigner everywhere,' her identity as a misfit—'I don't fit,/like a clumsily—translated poem ...' (101) is a manifesto of separation and distancing from ethnic identities: All kinds of places and groups of people who have an admirable history would, almost certainly, distance themselves from me (Minority, 101).

The poet's mandate comes from 'certain certainties' about the right path and right action. The path, one of justice, human rights and an inclusive subjectivity, widens into the expanse of an intersubjectivity, that erases the divide between the self and the other constructed in religious, cultural, and national terms. Dharker's reflective persona in the poem 'Minority,' shares the transformative moment in the following lines: 'until one day, you meet the stranger sliding down your street, realize you know the face simplified to bone, look into its outcast eyes and recognize it as your own' (103).

In the political and existential battle being waged in contemporary societies between forces of regulation and freedom, Dharker seizing the advantage of interstitial spaces, generates the evolutionary consciousness linking intersubjectivities, reviving a rhythmic connection with the universe, while keeping her ear to the ground for inhuman, discordant voices. Her projection of multiple subjectivities is a mapping of a highest evolving state of consciousness, affirmed through the 'liminality' of her poems.

The speaking subject in Dharker's poems stands in a dialogic relationship to reality. As Holquist states, 'Dialogism begins by visualizing existence as an event, the event of being responsible for (and to) the particular situation existence assumes, as it unfolds in the unique (and constantly changing) place I occupy in it' (Holquist, 2002).

Poetry, in Dharker's craftsmanship, a powerful vibration of speech and voice, exposes the autocracy of power-centric groups and institutions, linking the subjectivities of the margins of undiscovered truths, of silences, of the dissenting mind, the choked imagination. Her poems demonstrate the inherent possibilities for defeating the game play of identity appropriation and construction in the contemporary world, precipitated by immigration, fundamentalism and sophisticated electronic surveillance.

Fulfilling the condition of 'the liminality of cultural identity' envisioned by Bhabha, in Dharker's poems, a 'gathering' of experiences and insights take us to the necessity of fusing prepositional categories of 'mine' and 'yours', working out new paths of belongingness. Shifting the centre of awareness beyond the Muslim women's identity of the *Purdah* poems, Dharker locates herself within the critical yet compassionate interstitial space: 'For it is by living on the borderline of history and language, on the limits of race and gender, that we are in a position to translate the differences between them into a kind of solidarity' (Bhabha, 170). Dharker's achievement lies in engagement with acts of discovery, constantly questioning identity and subjectivity in relational and transactional encounters in the contemporary world. Delivered through poignant and incisive images and voices, her often bardic, poetic mandate captures the journey of the expanding 'I' of the self-responding sensuously, emotionally and imaginatively to the threat to the human.

REFERENCES

Bhabha, Homi K. "DissemiNation: Time, Narrative and the Margins of the Modern Nation," in *Nation and Narration*, Ed. Homi K. Bhabha, London and New York: Routledge, 1990, pp. 291–322.

Blommaert, Jan. *Discourse.* Cambridge: Cambridge University Press, 2005.

Dharker, Imtiaz. *I Speak for the Devil* (2001). New Delhi: Penguin Books, 2003.

— *Postcards from God*. New Delhi: Viking Penguin, 1994.

— *Purdah*. Three Crowns: OUP, 1989.

— *The Terrorist at my Table* (2006). New Delhi: Penguin Books, 2007.

Fludernik, Monika. "The Constitution of Hybridity: Postcolonial Interventions", in *Hybridity and Postcolonialism: Twentieth-Century Indian Literature* (1998). Ed. Monika Fludernik. Jaipur: Rawat Publications, 2006.

Glover, David and Cora Kaplan (2000). *Genders*. London and New York: Routledge, 2001.

Harting, Heike. "Subjectivity," in *Globalization and Autonomy Glossary,* 2005. http://anscombe.mcmaster.ca/globalization.

Holquist, Michael. *Dialogism* (1990). London and New York: Routledge, 2005.

Jameson, Fredric and Masao Miyoshi. Ed. *The Cultures of Globalization.* Durham and London: Duke University Press, 1998.

Kakar, Sudhir and Katharina Kakar. *The Indians: Portrait of a People.* New Delhi: Penguin Viking: 2007.

Parameswaran, Uma. *Writing the Diaspora*. Jaipur: Rawat Publications, 2007.

Proctor, Jones. Ed. *Writing Black Britain.* Manchester: Manchester University Press, 2000.

Robbins, Bruce. "Race, Gender, Class, Postcolonialism: Toward a New Humanistic Paradigm?" *A Companion to Postcolonial Studies* (2000). Ed. Henry Schwarz and Sangeeta Ray. USA: Blackwell Publishing, 2005.

Spivak, Gayatri Chakravarty. "Questions of Multi-culturalism: A Dialogue with Sneja Gunew," *The Post-colonial Critic: Interviews, Strategies, Dialogues*. Ed. Sarah Harasym. New York and London: Routledge, 1990.

Wikipedia. http://en. Wikipedia.org/wiki/Intersubjective12/12/08 http://en. Wikipedia.org/wiki/Interstitial_art12/12/08.

CHAPTER 10

Childhood Ghosts and the Scars of Adulthood

Lamming's *In the Castle of My Skin*

Urmil Talwar

Reflexive thought is the distinguishing mark of human beings that allows them to think about their past as also about who they are and how they are perceived by others. Accordingly individuals are constantly redefining the 'self', a symbolic construct that reflects their consciousness and their identity. Although the 'self' is perceived to reflect uniqueness,[1] it is influenced by culture and relationships with family, friends and social groups. The individual self, the relational self, and the collective self, interacting with one another help in defining the self-concept.[2] The self-concept is also influenced by the sense of identity formed in contradistinction to the claims of other groups to a similar sense of uniqueness, so that in real sense identity formation or the self-concept is a relational and comparative phenomenon locked into 'we/they' or 'self/other' antipathies. To belong to a group is simultaneously to include and exclude, to establish a boundary, even though this line of demarcation may be a fluid and situational social construct. Identity/self-concept is neither static nor eternal in its constitution, it is rather profoundly dynamic and always in a state of flux, in the process of 'becoming'.

Since childhood individuals unconsciously start collecting, reflecting and selecting the past memories. These childhood memories leave an indelible impression on the individual and at a later stage the individual explores these influences that have shaped his present. These form the memoirs or the autobiographies of the individuals. In this paper I propose to explore the formation of the self-concept/identity through the experience of George Lamming, an Afro-Caribbean writer in his fictional autobiography *In the Castle of My Skin*. Lamming's autobiography is neither a confession nor an instruction for life; it is but a reflection about life. It weaves in and out of conflicts that allow no resolutions. I will also discuss the formation of Afro-Caribbean identity as revealed in the colonial encounters. Interweaving the reflective thought in autobiography with those of postcolonial the paper brings out the dialectical relationship between the self and the other, the inside and the outside, the master and the slave, the colonizer and the colonized.

In The Castle of My Skin, the *magnum opus* of George Lamming is a disguised autobiography and the author acknowledges in *The Pleasures of Exile* that certain facts contained in this novel are closely linked to his childhood experiences (226). A classic among the childhood novels in Caribbean literature, it is a journey of the inner consciousness that reflects the personal and artistic life of the author through a backward glance. Published in 1953 at the high noontide of the struggle against colonialism, it not only recounts the personal life of the author but also the various social, economic and political changes taking place in the society, and it makes a sustained attack on colonial administrative system, the imperial economic system, the colonial educational institutions, the language, colour, class, race, and all that affects the life of the young in formative years.

The Caribbean author takes on a variety of techniques to explore his former status of a colony. He seeks to express how the political and cultural hegemony of Europe has affected their psychology. To relate the experience of colonial oppression as felt by both individual and community Lamming uses multiple narrative perspectives in his novel. In the introduction to *In the Castle of My Skin*, he indicates that British colonialism had created a fragmented society torn between its desire to emulate the 'Mother' country and the need to establish an independent existence. The result was:

> ... A fractured consciousness, a deep split in sensibility which now raised different problems of language and values; the whole issue of cultural allegiance between imposed norms of White Power, represented by a small numerical minority, and the fragmented memory of the African masses: between White instruction and Black imagination (xxxvii).

Lamming reveals this colonial experience through three narrative vehicles. First, 'the personal self' is constructed through first person autobiographical account of the character of G.; secondly, 'the relational self' is constructed through a third person account of the conversation between the Old Man (Pa) and the Old Woman (Ma). Thirdly, 'the collective self' includes construction through the third person account that relates broader events of the village as a whole. Haunted by the childhood memories Lamming frames the novel by the narrative of G. This allows Lamming to credibly relate how an individual comes to know himself—the reader gains an understanding of how G. recognizes the shaping effect of British colonialism on his 'self'. The novel begins on a very personal and ironic note. The ninth birthday of the narrator, George, ruined by rain and God's 'shower of blessings', has turned into deluge that washes away houses, and disrupts, distorts and dislocates the life of villagers. The torrential rain and the ensuing flood symbolically reveal the chaos and the inner flood of emotions, '... our lives—meaning our fears and their corresponding ideals—seemed to escape down an imaginary drain that was our future' (10). The water imagery at the very outset symbolizes the time of change and evokes the imagery of legendary waters that set a curse on the course of man. The weather sets the tone and hints at the future course of events.

The note of rootlessness and restlessness are struck at the very beginning as a prelude to the understanding of inner flood of emotions due to a total lack of familial relations. George says, 'My parents on almost all sides had been deposited in the bad or uncertain accounts of all my future relationships and loneliness from which had subsequently grown the consolation of freedom was the legacy with which my first year opened' (12). G. has been raised primarily by his mother, his father had left before he was born, his uncle had gone to US to find work, his grandmother lived in Panama, his grandfather died many years before. The effects of colonialism—the poverty and consequent premature death, families torn apart by lack of opportunity, and the prevalent British customs and decorum—are all detailed by G. in the first chapter. His mother had always diverted him from searching his roots/identity, revealing the attitude of the villagers at large who had not bothered at all about their own history. The binary opposites 'loneliness' and 'freedom' representing colonized and decolonized states of the individual and the society are juxtaposed throughout the novel. The second chapter describes the hierarchical structure with landlord at the top, followed by layers of overseers and underlings and at the lowest level are G.'s friends and neighbours, 'My people are low-down nigger people' (26). G. remembers his pal Boy Blue explaining: 'Just as I was going to be born the light went out.' And Lamming himself testifies:

> No black boy wanted to be white, but it was also true that no black boy liked the idea of being black. Brown skin was a satisfactory compromise ... . The best looking girls in the village were those whose mother had consorted with white men.

Later in the novel, G. relates his contacts with the white inhabitants of Barbados.

> We were now in Belleville where the white people lived, and the streets bordered by palm trees were called avenues. Here the houses were all bungalows high and wide with open galleries and porticoes. Bottles of milk were grouped on the steps, and occasionally light flickered from the kitchens where the servants were preparing early coffee. (109)

With his friends Trumper, Blue Boy and Bob, G. views the White world as it entertains itself. As he watches them dance in the landlord's house, G. envies the sailors and wonders what it would be like to hold a woman. When the boys are discovered and chased off the property by the Black overseer, they seek refuge among a crowd of evangelicals. This scene is symbolic as in colonial societies oppressed people frequently turn to religion for protection from their tormentors. Beyond its spiritual comfort, the church becomes a site of communal strength and resistance. The boys have lengthy conversations about the frustrations of life, the peculiar institution of marriage, their position in the world. Even at these moments, the British influence—or indoctrination—is felt.

The primary object of the novel is George's initiation to life but this gets clouded by the global mutations taking place in the community, the village, the country and at the international level. The description and the importance accorded to the school, the church and the house of the landlord/the castle on the hill depict how the British colonial rule percolates to the masses. The ties between the colonizer and the colonized can be summed up from the statement, 'They got up in the morning to landlord's bell and go to bed when the lights on the house on the hill go out' (29).

The castle is the central image of the novel. In *The Pleasures of Exile* (228), Lamming explains that he has taken this from Derek Walcott's poem in which the persona addresses the white persons separated from him by colour and class: You in the castle of your skin/I among the swineherd.

But Lamming changes the possessive pronoun reversing the entire situation and seizing the castle for himself and placing the Black peasant in the castle of his skin, as the proverb goes 'the Englishman's home is his castle', thereby restoring some dignity to the black identity, since the Black skin is the only castle that he possesses. The Black skin with its connotations of exposure, shame and deprivation are transformed into an image of impregnability, strength and self-sufficiency.

The castle at first is introduced as a political metaphor when Creighton's house on the top of the hill is described, 'It was a castle around which land like a shabby black garden stretched' (29). The landlord and his relationship to the village are revealed in terms of medieval roles of master and slave. This relationship changes by the end of the novel when Creighton and his castle are replaced by Mr Slime's land consortium.

A symbol of isolation, the castle is impregnable at the beginning, not allowing access to those who are curious about its interior designs. Lamming uses this imagery to preserve the integrity and identity of the individual. Castle building is a natural part of child's play in the village, and in the novel children build sand castles on the sea beach, which is a group effort that unites its members, even as it isolates them. Lamming uses it as a symbol both of individual strength and group unity. When George prepares to leave the village, he records:

> I am always feeling terrified of being known; not because they really know you, but simply because their claim to this knowledge is concealed attempt to destroy you … . They can never know you … . They won't know the you that's hidden somewhere in the castle of your skin (261).

Not only George or Lamming but all Caribbean diaspora writers were padlocked within the castle of their skin; they were imprisoned within racial garrisons. They had a tendency to write for or on behalf of narrow racial groups, their eyes glazed over different nostalgias for racial beginnings outside the Caribbean. When George, the narrator, looks back for history, he finds indignity, when he gropes for tradition he found it fragmented, and his quest for mythology led to the Gods of his primitive religion. For history, tradition and mythology he had to fall back on the European. The writers of African descent wrote for those who shared their racial heritage and availed of the first opportunity to go to England and there was a mass departure of writers from West Indies—Jean Rhys, Lamming, Naipaul and others. To fight cultural imperialism, Fanon wrote in 'On National Culture' one must write about one's own culture and look for strength of his own roots, his history and his destiny and turn English language into an anti-language experience (192–195). English education is also an intellectual's castle from which escape is difficult and painful but not impossible. It is expected that those who escape may return to liberate the others. Most of the Caribbean writers who had migrated to England should have returned with an intense commitment to Caribbean community. Lamming does not merely gripe about the legacy of the past, he rather seeks empowerment by using his work as a vehicle to deconstruct damaging assumptions. He explores the process of cultural mixture and toys with the notion of centre/margin.[3]

The movement of George from Barbados to Trinidad and further to England marks a shift from margin to the centre. The centre formed by Ma and Pa, the oldest and the unnamed characters, respected by everyone as the elders of the village, shifts to the margin with the movement of Pa to the Alms House. In *The Pleasures of Exile* Lamming writes:

> When I was 12 years old I had the shattering experience of seeing old papa Grandison, my Godfather, forced to move his small house from the site which generations of children had learnt to speak of as the corner where Papa who keeps the goats live … . Papa's rock had been taken, his castle ignored; but Papa would always remain. That journey was a lesson in exile and permanence; that night was a colonial example of alienation. It must have been the origin of that farewell which Papa and I bade each other … the book which was built on this rock (228).

This also explains the meaning of the statement, 'Papa's departure is the story of *In the Castle of My Skin.*' From beginning to end, Ma and Pa represent 'tradition and stability', the rock of peasant consciousness. Pa's forced withdrawal symbolizes the elimination of a generation, which would have been the spiritual conscience of the new society. Lamming was deeply moved by the Black Barbados peasants because they were not only poor but also forced off the land in 1930s on which they had lived and worked for generations. Lamming relates this part of the story through the third person accounts of the British school worker's strike, the riots that spread from the city to the village, the evictions carried out by the new landowners, and the conversations between Ma and Pa. In contrast to the young narrator, Ma and Pa, serving as the living memory of the village's past, are approaching the end of their lives.

The tragic sense of alienation and dispossession is caught in a moment of parting with the mentor when George wins a scholarship and George says, 'The earth where I walked was a marvel of blackness and I knew in a sense more deep than simple departure I had said farewell, farewell to the land' (303). It was a farewell not only to land but also to the people, to places, and to the way of life.

George's education and his language too becomes his castle. Language becomes both a vehicle for assimilation, a defense weapon and a tool for empowerment. Lamming uses the third person narrative to introduce the colonial system of education. The schools were structured exactly as they were in Britain, with no regard for the needs or interests of the Black pupils in Barbados or elsewhere in the Caribbean. He takes up the issue of education both at an individual and at political level. At personal level he narrates his individual experiences. George's mother makes him compete for Exhibition Scholarship and for this she makes sacrifices to pay for 3–4 years' special tuition fee to qualify him for entry into a prestigious High School. George is constantly aware of the sacrifices she has made and later describes them in his dairy as 'an unbearable monologue'. His mother makes the choice for him and George understands that she wishes to alienate him from his peasant origins. Though George is perceptive enough to recognize the value his mother places on his success, which promises social and material success and advancement, it is at the school that he understands that their Blackness is associated with their being at the base of the social pyramid. School becomes a symbol of cultural conflict.

At the political level Lamming perceives school and formal education as colonial tools. Through education it was emphasized that European civilization was paramount and all that was Black and local was disparaged. The novel analyses the process by which children are socialized to endorse colonial values whereby colonial and peasant sensibilities are diametrically opposed. George is torn apart by this painful dichotomy, a division within the self. In the novel the village life and school life do not overlap. George finds his village friends drifting away as he becomes immersed in the activities and attitudes of the school. Allegorically, the foreign influences attempt to lead George away from his traditional culture by making him subservient to alien faith that proves to be the source of conflict in young boy. Suspended between the two worlds, he says, 'It was as though my roots had been snapped from the centre of what I knew best, while I remained impotent to wrest what my fortunes had forced me into' (220). George felt that he was psychically fragmented and culturally schizophrenic reflecting the condition of the society as a whole. While formal education serves to alienate peasant children from their background, it nonetheless promises such social and material advancement that matters. In its anxiety to maintain its hold on the colonized the Empire had developed stereotypes, which taught disrespect to their own age-old ways of living, thinking and in their place proclaimed its civilizing mission. He sees education as a means of perpetuating and maintaining colonial authority, it is a tool for instilling deference, submission and respect. In *The Pleasures of Exile,* Lamming examined the colonial past, decolonization and his own identity. He identifies himself with Caliban, Prospero's slave on a remote island in Shakespear's play, *The Tempest*.

The friendship between George and Trumper is of great significance and assumes political dimensions. It is through Trumper that Lamming raises another aspect of race consciousness. After Trumper's return from America, in the last chapter of the novel, G. is made to realize that the castle is not merely a place to hide but also a place to locate oneself and look upon the world. It is Trumper who perceives how the game of selling and buying land is being played. He criticizes Slime's undertaking and proposes a boycott of land transfer from colonizer to local bourgeoisie. The author expresses his ideas about colonialism through Trumper. After his journey to US and suffering racial tension there Trumper's message becomes pan-African and is supported by recorded music of the Black, Paul Robeson, 'Let my people go.' He advocates the united struggle of the dispossessed. Ngugi Wa Thiong'O writes:

> When Trumper comes back, he has a better grasp and appreciation of the situation in Barbados. Exile is both a spiritual and physical state. Emigration becomes the symbol of struggling West Indian alienated from his past and immediate world (125).

He brings a new level of thinking to bear on the situation of the village, in this way deepening their already awakened consciousness. In Lamming's view, exile gave Trumper the perspective needed to judge accurately the nature of change in Barbados. After his contact with the Black American nationalists, Trumper identifies with the oppressed Blacks (293), and this enables him to appreciate the international character of the problems, which beset his own country (295). Trumper also warns G. of what his own terrible and proud future will be when one day he too goes much farther than Trinidad and learns about race. G. has a feeling of sickness and he begins to understand Trumper's commitment 'to fight for the rights of Negroes and to die fighting' (297).

Lamming records the major events of the West Indian history, the massive migration of 1930s, the demand for decolonization during late 50s and the tension and implications which have transpired within the society subsequent to independence (Yarde, 36). For Lamming the historical events provide support only for imaginative work. The maintenance of the diary and his continuous reading of it, despite his mother's disapproval, is a symbolic rebirth for George, who can no longer be the child his mother wants him to be. The novel concludes, taking us back to George's own thoughts:

> The village/my mother/a boy among boys/a man who knew his people won't feel alone/to be a different kind of creature. Words and voices falling like a full shower and the old man returning with the pebbles under the grape leaf on the sand. You won't see me again, my son. (303)

Lamming in his desire to demonstrate the complex cultural and political shifts in the community imposes an adult perspective on the boy's consciousness, defeating the notion of fidelity to childhood experience. Alfred Adler (1937) made this point about our earliest recollections: that they represent the current 'life style' of the individual, and serve to remind the person of who he or she is. Adler thus reverses the Freudian view of causation: childhood memories don't determine adult personality; rather adult personality determines what will be remembered from childhood. More recently, Michael Ross (1989, 1994) has argued that people construct their personal histories around tacit theories of the self, and revise these histories as their self-concepts change.[4] Paul Pickrel in a review in *The London Times* wrote: Lamming appears to have been unable to make up his mind whether to explore the world of adolescent consciousness or the world of social history, he has tried to make the best of both (406–419).

The search for identity is the major theme of Lamming's fiction and he uses details from his own autobiography *In The Castle of My Skin* to get at the root of the Caribbean soul. George's personal experience crystallizes the experience of the entire community. In a sense he is the village; the history of his dislocation echoes the dislocation of the village. He is a collective character (Pacquet, 14). Along with V.S. Naipaul, he is one of the exponents of the Caribbean renaissance that took place in England. Classed with other political authors like Vic Reid, Wilson Harris, Everton Weekes, Derek Walcott, Garfield Sobers, he is credited for making the emergence of Caribbean identity possible. Lamming feels that the lack of cultural identity is a direct result of the history of colonial rule.

Endnotes

1. A milestone in the development of self-concept theory was the writing of Sigmund Freud (1900) who gave us new understanding of the importance of internal mental processes. While Freud and many of his followers hesitated to make self-concept a primary psychological unit in their theories, Freud's daughter Anna (1946)

gave central importance to ego development and self-interpretation. By far the most influential and eloquent voice in self-concept theory was that of Carl Rogers (1947) who introduced an entire system of helping built around the importance of the self. In Rogers' view, the self is the central ingredient in human personality and personal adjustment. Rogers described the self as a social product, developing out of interpersonal relationships and striving for consistency. He maintained that there is a basic human need for positive regard both from others and from oneself. He also believed that in every person there is a tendency towards self-actualization and development so long as this is permitted and encouraged by an inviting environment.

2. The 'individual self' or 'the personal self-concept' consists of attributes and personality traits that differentiates one from other individuals and has some sort of comprehension of her or himself as a discrete, separate entity. 'The relational self" or the 'social self-concept' is a sense of affiliation, of relationships with significant others and of continuity, and the 'collective self' or the 'social ideals' is a sense of belonging to a group (the collective) that is so strong that a person who identifies with the group will dedicate his or her life to the group over individual identity: he or she will defend the views of the group and assume risks for the group, sometimes as great as loss of life. See Wikipedia on 'self' and 'self-concept'.
3. The landlord, symbolic of the British empire stays within his own safe ground, resting on his family name and reputation and remaining blind to whatever is going on around. As Bhabha describes it in the *Location of Culture* the Third Space (Inbetween or liminal) is a space where neutrality becomes effective (34-38). This Third Space is the threshold of cultural and ethnic otherness to grow and prosper. It is a space where cultural difference is not only tolerated and appreciated as a viable space for togetherness, but is deferred continually, and its border pushed backwards to offer a margin for survival. The traditional centre is his portrayal of the landlord, the wealthy estate owner who conspicuously remains absent throughout the novel.
4. Excerpts from Adler and Michael Ross have been quoted as in John F. Kihlstrom's essay 'Memory, Autobiography, History'.

REFERENCES

Adler, A. (1937). "The Significance of Early Recollections". *International Journal of Individual Psychology, 3*, 283–287.

Fanon, Frantz. "On National Culture" in *The Wretched of the Earth*. Middlesex: Penguin Books, 1963.

Kihlstrom, John F. "Memory, Autobiography, History", in *Proteus: A Journal of Ideas*. Special issue on Memory, Vol. 19, No. 2, Fall 2002.

Lamming, George. *In The Castle of My Skin* (1953).Essex: Longman Drumbeat,1983.

—. *The Pleasures of Exile*. London: Michael Joseph Ltd.,1960.

Pacquet, Sandra. *The Novels of George Lamming*. London: Heinmann Educational, 1982.

Pickrel, quoted from Ambroide Kom, "*In the Castle of My Skin*. George Lamming and the Colonial Caribbean". *World Literature Written in English*. Vol. 18, No. 2, Nov. 1979, pp 406–419.

Thiong'O, Ngugi Wa, *Homecoming*, London: Heinmann,1983.

Yarde, Gloria, "George Lamming: The Historical Imagination", in *The Literary Half Yearly* 11 (July 1970).

CHAPTER 11

Self/Selves?

Voices in the Construction of *Alias Grace*

Sudha Shastri

Some of the issues in considering the representation of the self in *Alias Grace* are anticipated, even determined by Margaret Atwood herself; her 'letter to the reader' and her interview are two instances. Her main concern is the lack of definitive material about the life of Grace Marks. The mainspring of the story came from Susanna Moodie's *Life in the Clearings* (1853), which was itself problematical. To quote Atwood:

> But she wrote it, as she says, from memory, and she got a lot of it wrong, as I found when I went back to the actual newspapers of the time and went into things such as the prison records. It always bothered me that the story Moodie told was so theatrical. It made you wonder, could it really have been like that? And when I went back to check, in fact, it wasn't. She had done a certain amount of embroidery.

In her letter she says:

> Years passed and Grace Marks continued to wander around in my head. I wrote a script about her for a television play. More time passed and she kept insisting on being given a fuller hearing, so I began to write this novel. Was Grace Marks the cunning female demon many considered her to be—or was she simply a terrorized victim? I began researching not only the murder case but life in Victorian times. Every major element in the book was suggested by something in the writing about Grace and her times, however suspect such writing might be; in gaps left unfilled, I was free to invent. Since there were a lot of gaps, there is a lot of invention.

And she ends her letter with this invitation to the reader:

> I invite you to meet ALIAS GRACE. May she stop wandering around in my head, and perhaps wander around in yours for a while.

Atwood's wish has certainly come true at least for us, the present reader and writer. Grace Marks, angel or monster? This question, which pertains to the crux of selfhood and identity, and is also a Victorian question, is nuanced brilliantly in *Alias Grace*.

The Story

Grace Marks of the title is an erstwhile maid who has been convicted of abetting James McDermott in the murder of their former employer Thomas Kinnear and his servant/mistress Nancy Montgomery. McDermott is hanged for his crime, but Grace is pardoned on account of her tender youth, and imprisoned in Kingston Penitentiary. A brief spell of psychological disorder/insanity is also attributed to her. When the novel begins, Dr Simon Jordan asks to meet Grace, with a view to finding if she was innocent or guilty.

Some Issues

The story of Grace Marks is as much a prototypical story of a woman of her situation (an unusual one no doubt) in the Victorian period, as of the individual herself. In fact, as Atwood points out, she has to depend on the milieu in constructing the self of Grace Marks, thereby making selfhood dependent on the milieu and times. This is particularly apposite in Grace's case as the science and spiritualism of the times go a considerable distance in shaping perceptions of her.

Significantly enough, Grace, as she emerges in Atwood's representation, is as much a self created by the people she interacts with, as 'her own person'. Her outpourings rarely work as therapy or catharsis; instead, in one telling episode, the questions that Dr Jordan puts to her slant the situation towards voyeurism, as Grace herself recognizes and protests against. And at the end of a long narrative, Grace still retains the answer to the question of her innocence or guilt: a single definitive

Grace eludes the reader tantalizingly/annoyingly, depending on how ready the reader is to accommodate doubt. Questions that the novel throws up are: how distant is the *narrating* self from the *narrated* self? Or, to include a more pertinent category, from a *perceived* self?

When confronted with her conflicting statements of confession, Grace reveals that she had been instructed by the lawyer to say so-and-so or such-and-such; a case of the self produced by a circumstance. She tells 'us' that her lawyer 'had told them' that she was 'next door to an idiot', (23–24) which angered her, until she is advised by her lawyer that it was her best chance; it would not be a good idea for her to appear too intelligent (the historical and cultural context determining the self). Our early encounter with Grace Marks sees her disputing the ways in which she is represented:

> The reason they want to see me is that I am a celebrated murderess. Or that is what has been written down. When I first saw it I was surprised, because they say Celebrated Singer and Celebrated Poetess and Celebrated Spiritualist and Celebrated Actress, but what is there to celebrate about murder? (23)

A little later:

> I think of all the things that have been written about me—that I am an inhuman female demon, that I am an innocent victim of a blackguard forced against my will and in danger of my own life, that I was too ignorant to know how to act and that to hang me would be judicial murder, that I am fond of animals, that I am very handsome with a brilliant complexion, that I have blue eyes, that I have green eyes … .(23)

This kind of displaced description sets the tone for the rest of the novel, ensuring that the distance between Grace and the reader is never bridged. It is noteworthy that the accounts are mutually inconsistent and conflicting.

Access to Grace Marks

Atwood's interrogation of assumptions within the discourse of personal disclosure contributes a sense of adventure to the reading of *Alias Grace*: Grace's rendering of her story is layered by more than one (her own) perspective. On the one hand, her narration takes place within the framework of a two-part discourse: she has an audience in Dr Simon Jordan, and she is primarily addressing his curiosity in her as a scientific subject. Dr Jordan is Atwood's fictive creation; and surely by endowing him with the role of listener, Atwood problematises the act of self-expression. We get more than one indication that Grace is embroidering her story in accordance with Dr Jordan's wishful demands. Well into the novel we also have a suggestion from Grace's erstwhile lawyer that she could be prolonging the meetings with Dr Jordan as she enjoys his company.

If autobiography is confession, the basis of mutual trust that underlies any confessional outpouring is already subverted in Grace's narration through her remarks in aside, to herself/the reader. Mediation, dislodged in a typical outpouring of the self, is present in many ways in *Alias Grace*.

To recapitulate the voices in the construction of *Alias Grace*, we have the doctor's (usually in letters to his friends): a third-person point-of-view, wearing, for the most part, the doctor's lenses; and Grace's voice, on two levels: one where she narrates to Dr Jordan, within the frame of a dialogue; and the other where the reader becomes privy to Grace's reflections on how her audience conditions her story: 'Shall we continue with your story where we left off? he says ... I've forgotten just where that was, I say. This is not quite true, but I wish to see if he has really been listening to me, or just pretending to' (229).

Thus Grace has the advantage of Dr Jordan; just as eventually Grace will also have the advantage of the reader.

The varying levels of selfhood that Grace chooses to exhibit at different points in time confounds the truth-value of *Alias Grace*, as we see in one of the many instances that the novel offers. I have chosen one example from Chapter 28, where before launching on her story of the murder, Grace tells 'us' that Dr Jordan had been so thoughtful as to bring her a radish that she had asked for, and so she owed him an interesting story, something that would make him feel that his sessions with her were benefiting him professionally: 'Because he was so thoughtful as to bring me this radish, I set to work willingly to tell my story, and to make it as interesting as I can, and rich in incident, as a sort of return gift to him; for I have always believed that one good turn deserves another' (291).

There is some ambivalence in this remark, as to whether Grace intends to embroider the story or not. In all likelihood the ambivalence is intended. For it is marked enough to stand out from the ongoing level of definite information that Grace presents.

Belief, Credibility, Role-playing

This interplay of various voices constructing Grace's selfhood ranges across a wide spectrum; let us turn to the voices that construct her for more light. Dr Jordan's name comes to the fore, as do those of the other contenders to this post, whether the Reverend Verringer (who is disposed to see Grace as innocent, and is chairing a committee to prove this) or Dr Bannerling (who is convinced that Grace is a cunning murderess).

Dr Jordan does try hard to believe her. But it is no easy task. At one point he says he has come not to judge her but to see what she can remember (367), and assures her of his belief in her. But his control over his conversation with Grace is shown to be shaky as, with the progress of the interview, he finds Grace taking legitimate offence to his questions, and himself apologizing to her. The situation of which he was master at the beginning, gradually hands itself over to Grace.

Meanwhile, a furious debate is centred in the moments of unconsciousness and amnesia that Grace claims to have suffered during the time of the murders of Mr Kinnear and Nancy. This blank stretch invites others to make what they would of it, and deepen the conundrum. But has she really forgotten, or is she lying? We never know.

> What should I tell Dr Jordan about this day? Because now we are almost there. I can remember what I said when arrested, and what Mr

> MacKenzie the lawyer said I should say, and what I did not say even to him; and what I said at the trial, and what I said afterwards, which was different as well. And what McDermott said I said, and what the others said I must have said, for there are always those that will supply you with speeches of their own, and put them right into your mouth for you too; and that sort are like the magicians who can throw their voice, at fairs and shows, and you are just their wooden doll. And that's what it was like at the trial, … .(351)

Subsequently, the passage moves into the realm of questions, stylistically reinforcing the lack of clarity that the reader has to contend with.

And how are we meant to read Grace when she says: 'I *said* that I remembered some of the things I did. But there are other things *they said* I did, which I *said* I could not remember at all' (351 emphases added). One obvious question is, does Grace always tell the truth? The question rests. We have to rest with 'It might have happened' (352).

Elsewhere, she shows herself capable of playing a role: at the end of the novel, long after Dr Jordan has left the place, she tells the rest of her story assuming Dr Jordan to be a listener, locating herself in relation to him. Even within the story she tells him, she 'performs': speaking of how Janet, the Warden's daughter, announces her release to her, Grace declares that 'I could see that she felt some tears were in order, and I shed several' (528). Later she plays the role of a suffering victim who has to give pardon, when her husband Jamie Walsh requires this of her. In a word, she plays to her audience.

Of the various details given to us about her, the oft-presented is that Grace is a consummate artist, a craftswoman with an eye for visual appeal, as her detailed descriptions of the various quilts testify. It requires no great leap of the imagination to wonder if Grace was fabricating her story as well, especially in the light of her 'aside's to the reader. In the words of Mackenzie, her lawyer, in conversation with Dr Jordan: 'Let me put it this way—did Scheherazade lie? Not in her own eyes; indeed, the stories she told ought never to be subjected to the harsh categories of Truth and Falsehood' (452). The onus is thereby transferred to the listener (Dr Jordan, the reader).

Grace's self-portrayal is thus neither unambiguous nor independent; propped as it is by many voices including her (Grace's) own, it enables Atwood to foreground the strategies, themselves, of assessment of personal disclosure.

Title

The 'alias' in the title is a pointer to the destabilizing of the self in the novel in many ways. In the most specific way, it refers to the 'alias' that Grace uses when she is arrested: when she gives her name as Mary Whitney. Listening to Grace tell her story, we find that Mary Whitney was the only human being who gave her warmth, love and hope, even if she did come to a tragic end herself.

The title complicates the identity of Grace Marks by prefixing 'alias' before her Christian name; in the normal course, where there was, say, a real name and a pseudonym, the 'alias' would follow the real name. Atwood's title seems to be severed in the middle and what we have left worth is the alias, the pseudonym. It also conveys a false notion that 'Grace' is the alias (the name that comes after) whereas the alias was really 'Mary' used by Grace Marks.

Almost at the end of the narrative, Dr Jordan acts on the ever-present possibility that Mary Whitney never did exist, and that she was a figment of Grace's imagination. He takes his opportunity to visit the Adelaide Street Methodist Church where he finds a small grey stone with just the name 'Mary Whitney', on it. Of course, Grace had told him that she could not afford anything beyond just a name for Mary when she died, so he is not totally unprepared for this. But it makes him wonder, too. For just as it seems that Mary Whitney's existence has been proved, it comes as a flash to Dr Jordan that nothing, after all, has been proved:

> What are such physical tokens worth? A magician produces a coin from a hat, and because it's a real coin and a real hat, the audience

> believes that the illusion too is real. But this stone is only that: a stone. For one thing, it has no dates on it, and the Mary Whitney buried beneath it may not have any connection with Grace Marks at all. She could be just a name, a name on a stone, seen here by Grace and used by her in the spinning of her story. She could be an old woman, a wife, a small infant, anyone at all. (465–66)

The reader's attention to the role of aliases in the novel is drawn once again when Jeremiah, the peddler, a man just about tolerated by the gentry, and who features in the trial by name in virtue of having sold shirts to Mr Kinnear, reappears after a period of disappearance as Dr Jerome DuPont, a self-styled trained neuro-hypnotist. We see him for the first time at the Governor's residence when the narrative chooses Dr Jordan's point-of-view on page 94. It is noteworthy that we meet the man Jeremiah in his assumed identity first. Not until Grace chances to meet him and recognize him with startled surprise (363), do we become privy to the knowledge that he is but Jeremiah under a new name. Having known Jeremiah from Grace's description, and Dr Jerome from Dr Jordan's grudging ceding of some scientific credentials to him, it takes some amount of re-adjustment for the reader to reconcile the two different people into one person.

While one effect, certainly, of this identity-switch is to spice the plot by twisting it in an unexpected direction, and another to make a fool of Dr Jordan, along with others, the most pertinent effect for the argument of my paper is that of showing—exhibiting—by example, the impossibility of recognizing the 'same' person when he chooses to take an alias; of course, Grace recognizes the doctor to be her old friend the peddler, but the way in which she achieves this recognition, long after Jeremiah and Dr Jerome have asserted their separate selves to Dr Jordan as well as the reader, is productive of a sense of re-cognition; an awareness of the extent to which an alias can differ from the self it is a part of. The only difference is that Mary Whitney lies in the consciousness of Grace Marks, in all probability, while Dr DuPont and Jeremiah are both publicly available.

The Verdict

The plot turns dramatic when towards the end of the novel, Dr DuPont decides to hypnotize Grace in the house of Mrs Quennell, in the presence of Dr Jordan, the governor's wife, her daughter Lydia, and Reverend Verringer, among others. Dr Jordan asks the hypnotized Grace questions pertaining to the murders of Kinnear and Nancy, but the proceedings become less and less scientific and progressively spiritualist as Grace, under the spell of the sleep induced in her, returns answers that are sexually coloured and provocative; statements, in short, of the sort that Mary Whitney would make.

Mrs Quennell who conducts séances begins to speak of spirits, and indeed there are also suggestive table-rappings, much to Dr DuPont's supposed despair; and soon enough Mrs Quennell's perspective comes to be upheld when Grace denies that she is Grace, and Dr Jordan guesses the voice to be that of Mary Whitney; who claims to have possessed Grace Marks during the time of the murders.

It is never made clear whether Jeremiah and Grace have, between them, decided to stage this interesting spectacle and get the last laugh over science. It is left to Dr DuPont to give a scientific explanation to what has happened, as also provide a tradition:

> There have been cases of this kind … Wakley of *The Lancet* has written extensively on the phenomenon; he calls it *double consciousness*, although he emphatically rejects the possibility of reaching the so-called secondary personality through Neuro-hypnotism, as there is too much chance of the subject's being influenced by the practitioner. (485–86)

Dr Jordan brings Puysegeur into the debate, Puysegeur who spoke of alternating states of consciousness, and Dr DuPont enlarges the argument to posit two different personalities cohabiting the body, which, by having two separate sets of memories, were two different individuals for all practical purposes. The point hinges on the fact that we are what we remember, to which

Dr Jordan adds the converse point of view: perhaps, he says, 'we are also—preponderantly—what we forget' (486).

In the best postmodern tradition, *Alias Grace* withholds a final answer to the question: is she or is she not guilty? This question, as I have tried to show so far, is the crux of Grace's identity. And although the events at Mrs Quennell's residence are raised by Grace's letter to Jeremiah, the text perplexes the reader by speaking of the event itself with pronounced ambivalence; alluding to people's wary behaviour to her post the hypnotism, Grace says: 'They will not speak about what was said on that occasion, as they are of the opinion that it might unsettle my reason; which I doubt would be the case' (508–509). Why would it not be the case? Because she was part of the show? Or is this an innocuous aside? We will never know.

Later, just before ending her letter, she refers to a button that Jeremiah had sent her. At least, she assumes that it was Jeremiah who had sent it, because it was the same pattern as the button he had once given her in Mrs Alderman Parkinson's. 'Perhaps there was another message in it also, as a button is for keeping things closed up, or else for opening them; and you may have been telling me to keep silent, about certain things we both know of' (512). She never ventures into the domain of explicit utterance, so that like Dr Jordan, and all those on the committee, the reader too can but continue to speculate.

If Grace meant to endlessly defer the unveiling of her 'real' self, by now she has successfully accomplished it through Dr Jordan, the only person who came to talk to her and to learn the truth. When the novel ends, Dr Jordan has lost whatever faith he might have once had in his ability to know for certain, as evinced in his letter to his friend Edward. Moreover the attempt to 'write' the story of Grace Marks within the borders unequivocally drawn by the discipline of science has resulted in a failure. Dr Jordan's exit from the story is accomplished unceremoniously, after a half-hearted adulterous affair he had with his landlady. Indeed, by the time the novel ends, Dr Jordan's objectivity itself is discredited, as he is shown to be increasingly obsessed with

Grace; first confusing Rachel, his mistress, for her, and later persisting in calling his affianced bride (whose name is 'Faith') by the name of Grace. Dr Jordan's mother interprets this as an 'understandable confusion as Faith is very close to it in concept' (515). But the reader knows otherwise.

Who Writes the Self?

This continual undercutting of one kind of knowledge with another, layering the narrative with irony, becomes an end in itself. There is a limit to what everyone knows, whether tentatively or with certitude. The limit ultimately precludes the understanding of Grace Marks' character. It keeps coming in the way of definitively writing the self.

Atwood uses the selfhood of Grace Marks to show that the self is constructed not just by oneself—whether through memory, amnesia, desire—but also by others. With Grace Marks this seems particularly the case. Grace's identity is drawn by people ranging from Susanna Moodie to Margaret Atwood herself; and Atwood herself takes help from her fictional creations as well as texts that have purportedly nothing to do with Grace, to draw a portrait. There are two epigraphs to the novel: one from Moodie and the other a basho poem: 'Come, see/real flowers/of this painful world'. Chapters employ epigraphs varying from poems by Dickinson and Browning (Robert) to the confession of Grace Marks as reported in the *Toronto Star and Transcript* to McDermott's statement to Kenneth MacKenzie, retold in Susanna Moodie's *Life in the Clearings*. The versions conflict and obfuscate rather than clarify. And the poetic excerpts encourage an abstract metaphorical view of love, dreams, pain, and identity.

The related question, how much of recollection is really construction, fundamental to all First-Person narratives, is foregrounded in *Alias Grace* through the central character of the protagonist. When set in the context of a larger perspective, this becomes a rhetorical question that displaces the issue of reliability with that of the imagination, its power and its use as therapy. The power of the imagination becomes most marked in the narrative when insights come from the realm of dream rather than that of everyday reality. Dr Jordan 'is used' by Atwood to show the insidious power of mental preoccupation that can confuse identities/selves in states of unusual consciousnesses. Grace has several dreams, mostly of a symbolic nature. Significantly, the most crucial moments in her life, the moments that shape her identity as murderess, are lost in the world of dreams and unconsciousness. Questions regarding the authenticity of the narrative also arise from Grace's moments of 'unconsciousness'. She can't remember, she says, what happened after Nancy was killed by McDermott, and the sequence of events that follow immediately thereupon are narrated by others: Jamie Walsh and the butcher. Does Grace use wayward memory as an escape from being implicated?

When Grace talks, Dr Jordan is the person who writes, not just by literally making notes, but also by drawing her out in a certain way, asking questions that tend in certain directions. His meetings with Grace inform his imagination so much so that her story and his understanding gradually part ways. Insofar as whoever has the power to represent has the upper hand in the telling of a story, Dr Jordan brings to life a Grace who constantly eludes.

REFERENCES

Atwood, Margaret. *Alias Grace*. Seal Books, 1996. Book Group Corner.
http://www.randomhouse.com/resources/bookgroup/aliasgrace_bgc.html 18 July 2006.

Life in the Clearings versus the Bush, by Susanna Moodie http://www.gutenberg.org/dirs/etext05/lcgbs10.txt 18 July 2006.

CHAPTER 12

Fictionalizing (Her) Self

Alice Munro's Short Stories

Bandana Chakrabarty

The 'self' is a key concept in several schools of psychology but in general, the self refers to the conscious, reflective personality of an individual. The self is a process of uncovering, discovering and re-discovering different layers to reach the core of one's very being. People remember what happened to them. These past events influence the present which is reconstructed by the person who experienced them. But how does a writer then 'define' or 'construct' his or her self in a literary text? Is it by writing a memoir, a confession or an autobiography? 'Confession,' says Francis Hart, 'is personal history that seeks to communicate or express the essential nature, the truth of the self'(491). Memoir, like confession, is a sub-category of autobiography. It is a piece of autobiographical writing, usually shorter in nature than a comprehensive autobiography. It may be more emotional and concerned with captivating particular scenes or a series of events rather than detailing every fact of life. Autobiography has received much attention in recent years. It presupposes that 'some shared identity bind author, narrator and character together' (Felski, 90). Lejeune defines 'autobiography' as 'a retrospective prose narrative produced by a real person concerning his own existence, focusing on his individual life in particular on the development of his personality' (193).

This paper seeks to examine some of the short stories of the Canadian writer Alice Munro—one of the world's best living short story writers, to show how in her writing, memory and imagination conjoin in an exploration of self-construction. The subject matter of Munro's stories has clearly developed from her own experience. Having explained in various interviews that her stories are not autobiographical, she claims an emotional reality for her characters that is drawn from her own life.

Born in 1931, Munro's life experiences of growing up in a relatively poor provincial southwest Ontario town during the Depression, negotiating the rebelliousness of adolescence, leaving home, studying at a university, falling in love, getting married, getting divorced, making a living by being a writer—all these construct the fiction that Munro writes. Munro analyses past experiences and reinvents them by experiencing them by living in the present. This she does with the help of memory. Memory is the way we keep telling ourselves our stories and telling other people a somewhat different version of our stories. Memory lies at the heart of both inner life and of human experience. Memory is both individual and collective and fictional narratives are practically inspired by these two types of memory. The psychologists and philosophers like Ricoeur believe that memory is a subjective experience and memories belong to the individual, helping to build identity by differentiating this individual from others.

Another school comprising Maurice Halbwachs and Joel Candau claim that all memory depends on the group in which one lives and to the status one holds in that group. But now there is an intermediary level of thought which holds that a writer belongs to a social group, shares a collective memory with it, and often deals in one's fictional works with a past pregnant with meaning which still impinges on the present. It is through the writing process that memory is constructed through which apparently lost memories can re-emerge. Marcel Proust considered the 'remembrance of things past' as inextricably linked to fiction writing.[1] Fiction does not have the obligation to tell the truth. Memory is selective; it cannot store all the elements of one's life. Neisser believes, 'The self that is remembered today is not the historical self of yesterday, but only a reconstructed version' (80). Munro, thus, achieves self-remembrance by a skilled use of narrative writing and a judicious use of the first-person as the subject in many of her stories.

In an interview with Metcalf, Munro said 'I use bits of what is real in the sense of being really there and really happening in the world as most people see it and I transform it into something that is really there and really happening in my story' (54). Munro readily admits that the raw material of her work comes from her own life. The act of writing about oneself is a way to find again that aspect of self and experience that may no longer be an actual part of one's life, but is a living memory shaping and informing the present. Munro's stories fictionalize the 'self' because they are wrought out of personal and often unconscious emotions; they fictionalize because the experiences have been transformed into the controlled discourse of art.

Munro herself favours a writing strategy which incorporates both the social and the autobiographical. In a meeting with Ding Ling, the Chinese radical feminist in 1981 Munro said, quoting Jean Rhys, 'I write about myself because I am the only truth I know.'[2] *Dance of the Happy Shades,* her first short story collection echoes Munro's childhood experience. Munro's father, Robert Laidlaw, was a fox farmer and she loved helping her father with the foxes and she was very proud of this. She says, 'I don't know why, but it was the first work I felt good about doing.' Of the first person reminiscences about childhood and adolescence 'Boys and Girls,' 'Day of the Butterfly,' 'Red Dress-1946' are seminal. In 'Boys and Girls' Munro records the humiliated and anguished psychology of a child who is being conditioned by society to become a definition—a *girl*. The girl finds herself no longer free to help her fox farmer father outdoors, but she is forced instead to take hold of her person in the conventional way by moving inside the home through housework. A gradual distance developed between the father and daughter. Munro writes, 'My mother was getting sick, so I had to go in and do housework which I always hated. It seemed tedious and the kitchen was dark and there was endless potato peeling and that sort of thing, and outside was all adventure.' The story 'Boys and Girls' describes this event thus: 'I was given jobs to do and I would sit at the table peeling peaches that had been soaked in hot water … . As soon as I was done I ran out of the house trying to get out of earshot before my mother thought of what she wanted me to do next' (*Dance,* 116–117).

The very first story in *Dance of the Happy Shades* entitled 'Walker Brothers' talks of the Depression of the 30s. The story comes from the actual experience of going with her father to visit a woman who teaches her to dance. Her father became a wandering salesman. The mother, on the other hand, took the initiative, had the fox skins made into fashionable fox headscarfs and easily sold them door-to-door. In 'Walker Brothers' since the father's business of fox farming failed he resorted to being a salesman selling cough medicine, iron tonic, corn plasters, laxatives, pills for female disorders, mouth wash, etc. Munro writes, 'Fate has flung us into a street of poor people and the only way to take this, as she sees it is with dignity, with bitterness, with no reconciliation' (*Dance,* 4). Munro has shown marks of that period's strain and depression in many of her stories. In *Lives of Girls and Women,* Del's mother, Addie Jordan goes from door-to-door selling encyclopedia and earning a living to help her family overcome the insoluble economic period. Munro's mother, Ann Laidlaw, actually sold furs to rich American tourists to stave off their financial disaster when her husband's fur-farming business received a jolt.

Using oneself as a first person narrator, Munro embarks upon her voyage of self-discovery. Names and locations are often changed and incidents are recreated to make them more dramatic but the story bears a close resemblance to that of the author. There is no pretence for neutrality. *Lives* have been identified as being based on her life. Munro, in defense, has asserted that it is autobiographical in some form but not entirely. Her narrators, whether it is Helen of *Dance of the Happy Shades* or Del Jordan of *Lives*, as filters of the past and present, possess an intelligence that makes one feel that if it's not her life being told then it is ours.

In Munro's world physical labour was considered as a test of worth. In her childhood her father raised mink and silver foxes, had horses, cows, sheep and a large vegetable garden, but they had no electricity, running water or indoor plumbing. This condition of theirs finds an echo in 'Ottawa Valley' where Munro writes, 'Our own house—which I always thought poor, because we lived too far out of town to have a flush toilet or running water, and certainly we had no real touches of luxury, like Venetian blinds—' (*Something,* 229–30). She had great respect for men and women with monotonous and ill-paid jobs. In 'The Turkey Season' (*Moons of Jupiter*) the characters make their living by killing and plucking, cleaning and packing birds for the Thanksgiving and Christmas market. They are proud of their strength, speed and skill. When the narrator, who has got a job at the Turkey Barn, sees turkeys hanging upside down, plucked and stiffened, she feels, 'I saw them not with aversion but with a sense of endless work to be done' (*Moons,* 61).

According to Munro's biographer, Robert Thacker, the sources of her literary power are grounded in a deep family connection to s. w. Ontario, where she was born. Many of her early stories take place in small towns and on farms in what is clearly s. w. Ontario. They are not literally true but as Munro has said, 'There has been a starting point in reality.' The area southwest of Toronto and east of Lake Huron is Alice Munro country. This place has been crucial to her. She said, 'It means something to me that no other country can, no matter how important historically that other country may be, how beautiful, how lively and interesting. I am intoxicated by this particular landscape. I speak the language'. Space has been a formative influence on Munro's imagination. She has evoked this place in several of her stories variously called Jubilee, Hanratty or Dalgleish. The town of Wingham has been immortalized in art. Munro has been successful in putting this 'intractably rural, unhurried and loconic region firmly on the literary map.'[3] Although a remote place, Thacker calls Munro's Huron Country 'a place remembered, recovered, revisited, and at times renounced' (214). In 'The Peace of Utrecht' the narrator puts it, as 'there is no easy way to get to Jubilee from anywhere on earth' (*Dance,* 196).

As a child, life at Lower Town School was miserable for Alice Munro. She describes those years at school as 'tumultous two years' (Ross). Later in a story called 'Privilege' (*Who*) Munro describes the protagonist Rose's schooling at a place very much like Lower Town School, 'Her schooling seemed deplorable .... But she was not miserable .... Learning to survive, no matter with what cravenness and caution .... It is not the same as miserable. It is interesting' (*Who,* 28). This is one story which Munro has called 'an autobiographical piece, not fiction at all' (Gerson, 4). Munro has drawn heavily on her childhood and adolescence in her fiction. Just as 'limited expectations and a pervasive self-effacing reticence' were the order of the day in the fictional town of Jubilee in her stories, Munro explained the reason for this thus: 'We were encouraged to be practical above everything. Self-fulfilling wasn't a concept' (Merkins).

Munro's mother features in many of her stories. *Lives of Girls and Women* deals with mother–daughter relationship in detail. Del realizes that she is in perpetual conflict with her mother because she is so much like her. Through her intelligence and educational opportunities Del has the chance to deviate openly from the social norms to escape from community and thus write her own story. When Alice Munro was a young girl her mother wanted her to learn to play tennis as a way of attracting men and moving up in the world, an idea she felt bound to reject along with most of her mother's ideas. The same ideas is reiterated in one of Munro's recent collections of stories titled *Runaway*. In the story 'Chance' the parents of the protagonist, Juliet, are proud of her possessing degrees in Classics. 'Her mother wanted her to be popular, and to that end had urged her to learn to skate and to play to the piano'

(*Runaway,* 53). Juliet did not do either willingly or well. Instead reading, and later, writing became a way of organizing the jumble of experience. Munro says 'I would even wash the dishes with a book propped up in front of me' {"Interview": Ross 5}. From the age of eleven, Alice made up stories in her head on the long walks to and from school. Writing provided a tremendous sense of joy and power. Lives is the chronicle of Del Jordan as she writes her own life story of growing up in Jubilee. Like Alice Munro, Del, too, wants to be a writer. Just as Lives chronicles Del's journey from an adolescent to being a writer, similarly three stories in the Runaway collection titled 'Chance', 'Soon', and 'Silence' depict the story of Juliet, a 21 year old girl in 1965 with a BA and MA in classics through some thirty years to where she is left off, short of money, and still studying 'the old Greeks' (*Runaway,* 158). Munro told Barbara Frum in an interview, 'I wanted to be a writer from the time I was 12, yet I never told anybody' (Ross, 19).

Tension between mothers and daughters allows to define their own boundaries more clearly. At the heart of mother-daughter relationship is ultimately identity crises. Suzanne Juhasz believes that to find her own identity, a daughter 'needs to ascertain the difference between herself and her mother'. 'For some women', notes Kathie Carlson, being like their mother is seen as 'equivalent to being powerless and trapped.' They do not wish to repeat their mother's actions or fulfil their mother's desires. Girls are valued according to their obedience, passivity and maintenance of the traditional ways. They resist any and all associations with the parental figure who is female. Despite years of caring and nurturing, the mother is visualized as a smothering figure, obtrusive and difficult. Subconsciously, the mother wants what is best for her daughter so that she has a life that is good and different from that of her own. In *Lives* Addie wants her daughter to have a good education and earn a scholarship, but Del rejects all her mother's values and wants to 'go out and take on all kinds of experiences and shuck off' what she didn't want and 'come back proud' (*Lives,* 173).

Women's literature in the past has dealt with 'matrophobia', that is, the fear of becoming one's mother. 'Hating one's mother was part of the feminist enlightenment of the Fifties and Sixties' (Showalter, 32). The conflict between mother and daughter eventually leads to some sort of separation. Critics like Kathie Carlson argue that the separation between the mother and daughter is necessary because the daughter identifies too greatly with her mother and will not have an opportunity to develop and identity of her own. She believes that matrophobia exists because the daughter 'unconsciously believes that if any part of her is like her mother, it will somehow reconstitute the whole ... she will lose her identity and become her mother.'

For Munro herself, the life and death of her mother is a central concern that is never far from her. When her mother contracted Parkinson's disease it fell to Munro, the oldest in the family, to keep the household running, an experience that completely shattered her. It made her tough and also damaged her relationship with her mother. 'My mother's illness frightened me so much that I couldn't identify with her. I learned to be capable simply because I had to be', she admits. She has said, 'My mother keeps cropping up in my stories.' Her mother died in 1959 and she went back to Wingham, her grandmother's house where she brought out her mother's clothes, an incident that became the core of 'The Peace of Utrecht,' a story in the first collection. Catherine Sheldrick Ross is of the view that 'this magnificent story was a breakthrough in terms of the use of personal material' (Ross, 29).

Some of the richest stories started from scenes in Munro's own life. 'Red Dress-1946' is concerned with her mother sewing her an elaborate dress. 'The Peace of Utrecht' is about Munro's experience of returning home after her mother's death, and being confronted with the 'invisible presence' of the mother. Munro calls them 'personal stories' because they draw on remembered and invented material—selected, reshaped and recombined—to convey an emotional reality that is close to Munro's own experience. After the publication of her third book, *Something I've been Meaning to Tell You* (1974), Kem Murch asked Munro about her talent for remembering the details of people's speech patterns, walk and stride, dress, weather, shadows and also if she took notes daily, Munro answered, 'They just come to me when I'm writing. It is a kind of seeing.' Munro's stories retain probability and authenticity while they delight the attentive reader with their functionality. Their realities are constructed of rare skill and masterful invention.

Munro's latest story collection *The View from Castle Rock* (2006) depicts seven generations of Munro's family history and culminates in her own. In the foreword she has written, 'I was doing something closer to what a memoir does—exploring a life, my own life.' she has kept herself at the centre and written about 'that self, as searchingly as I could.' But she instantly accepts that she has granted a freer existence to the ancestors, friends, relatives and lovers basing them on facts to some degree, but letting them do things 'they had not done in reality' (Shulevitz, 2). In two stories from *The View from Castle Rock* she treads familiar ground again. In 'The Hired Girl' Munro describes the unhappy summer of the protagonist as a maid to a rich family. Munro herself worked as a waitress in Muskoka Lodge while still at the University because her scholarship was not adequate to pay for her studies. Another story 'Working for a Living' shows her mother selling furs to rich women while her absence 'brought a sort of peace—not only between them (the parents) but for all of them,' admits Munro.

Although close to eighty, Alice Munro is still going strong with her creativity. Munro has proved that 'without the capacity to "carry the past with us" in some fashion, existence would indeed be short-lived' (Gergen, 100). Wandering back and forth is a way in which Munro's characters think about their social background, friends and even incidents in the past. She told Cara Feinberg in an interview, 'Time is something that interests me a lot—past and present, and how the past appears as people change.' Munro's stories follow the pattern of memory; they move forward and backward in time, just as memories do, and sometimes the earliest events in a story are narrated at the end. Till today Alice Munro has been feeling 'exultant about the choice' of choosing the life of a writer by fictionalizing her own life story.

Endnotes

1. Marcel Proust, *Remembrance of Things Past.* trans. C.K. Moncrieff and Terence Kilmartin, New York: Random House, 1981.
2. "A Conversation with Alice Munro" with John Metcalf. *Journal of Canadian Fiction* 1.4(1972): 54–62.
3. Quoted in W.R. Martin's *Alice Munro: Paradox and Parallel.* Edmonton: University of Alberta Press, 1987.
4. Alice Munro. "Great Dames." With Barbara Frum. *Maclean's. 1973: 32.*

REFERENCES

Carlson, Kathie. Quoted in "Matrophobia: The Search for a Daughter's Identity" Internet 22 October 2000. Available http://members.aol.com/deerskin/words/matrophobia.htm.

Feinberg, Cara "Bringing life to life" Dec.14, 2001. Internet Jan 7, 2002 Available http://www.theatlantic.com/unbound/interviews/int2001-12-14.htm.

Felski, Rita. *Beyond Feminist Aesthetics: Feminist Literature and Social Change.* Cambridge: Harvard University Press, 1989.

Gergen, Kenneth, "Mind, Text and Society: Self-memory in Social Context". *The Remembering Self: Construction and Accuracy in the Self-Narrative.* Cambridge: Cambridge University Press, 1994.

Gerson, Carole. "Review Interview with Alice Munro", *Room of One's Own* 4.4 (1979): 2–7.

Hart, Francis. "Notes for an Anatomy of Modern Autobiography," *New Literary History,* 1 (1970), p. 491.

Jusahz, Suzanne. "Matrophobia: The Search for a Daughter's Identity." Internet 22 October 2000. Available http://members.aol.com/deerskin/words/matrophobia.htm.

Lavenne, Francois Xavier, Viranie Renard and Francois Tollett "Fiction, between Inner Life and Collective Memory. A Methodological Reflection" in *The New Arcadia Review,* Vol. 3, 2005.

Lejune, Philippe. "The Autobiographical Contract", in *French Literary Theory Today: A Reader*, Ed. Tzvetan Todorov. Cambridge, Cambridge University Press, 1982, p.193.

Martin, W.R. *Alice Munro: Paradox and Parallel.* Edmonton: University of Alberlta Press, 1987.

Merkins, Daphne. "The Making of Alice Munro". www.theage.com.au/news/books/2004/11/25.

Metcalf, John. "A Conversation with Alice Munro" *Journal of Canadian Fiction* 1.4 (1972): 54–62.

Munro, Alice. *Dance of the Happy Shades.* (1968) London: Penguin, 1983.

— *Lives of Girls and Women.* (1971) London: Penguin, 1982.

— *Something I've Been Meaning To Tell You.* (1974) Toronto: Penguin, 1996.

— *Who Do You Think You Are?* Toronto: Penguin, 1978.

— *The Moons of Jupiter.* New York: Alfred Knopf, 1982.

— *Runaway.* Toronto: Penguin, 2004.

— *The View from Castle Rock.* Toronto: McClleland, 2006.

— *Great Dames.* With Barbara Frum. *Maclean's* Apr 1973: 32.

Murch, Kem. "Name: Alice Munro. Occupation: Writer". *Chatelaine 48.8* (August 1975): 69–71.

Neisser, Ulric and Robyn Fivush. *The Remembering Self: Construction and Accuracy in the Self-Narrative.* Cambridge: Cambridge UP, 1994.

Proust, Marcel. *Remembrance of Things Past.* trans. C. K. Moncrieff and Terence Kilmartin, New York: Random House, 1981.

Ross, Catherine Sheldrick. *Alice Munro: A Double Life.* Toronto: ECW Press, 1992.

Showalter, Elaine. "Towards a Feminist Poetics." *Women Writing and Writing about Women.* Ed. Mary Jacobus. London: Croom Helm, 1979.

Shulevitz, Judith. "The Anatomy of Destiny; Alice Munro, Spinner of Fates". http://www.slate.com/id/2151887.

Thacker, Robert. "Connection: Alice Munro and Ontario." *American Review of Canadian Studies* 14.2 (1984): 213–26.

CHAPTER 13

Unburying the Self ?

Confessions of Failure in Alice Munro

Nilofer Kaul

> *Exhibiting, baring, stripping down, unveiling—this is an old routine: the metaphor of truth* ... Jacques Derrida.[1]

In western discourse, the idea of confession has undergone several reincarnations from Augustine to Rousseau; however, for much of its history it has retained the notion of an essential self that cannot but must continue to search for its truth. This quest for the self was premised upon a polarization of public/private and apparent/real—often manifest in proverbial wisdom as: 'all that glitters is not gold', 'a goodly apple rotten at the core', 'don't judge a book by its cover'—endless platitudes reinforcing the difference between surface and depth, the shallow and the profound. Implicit in these polarized binaries would then be a privileging of the private over the public, and a belief that external reality often forbids expression of this inner, private experience. Interestingly, these assumptions ignored the fact that confession serves as a way of defining ourselves in accord with a social formation. According to Foucault, individuals police themselves by examining, confessing and regulating their own thoughts and behaviour in accord with a certain concept of normality. From the confessions made to the priest, to the ones made on the analyst's couch, and now in front of the TV audience, a confession requires active participation from the speaking subject. But what does it give to the listener?

While a confession ostensibly sought atonement, it tantalized the listener/reader with the fruit of forbidden knowledge—shame, sin, guilt or crime. In his comparison of Wordsworth's *Prelude* with Rousseau's *Confessions,* W.J.T. Mitchell observes, "Rousseau confesses everything and feels guilty for nothing, while Wordsworth confesses nothing and yet seems to feel excessive, unmotivated guilt for some unnamed crime" (614). This observation serves to indicate something fundamentally different between the two writers, yet what it also foregrounds is an unstated assumption that inevitably links guilt with confession. The one contains the promise of the other.

Such expectations have framed the western tradition of confession writing. A confession must repose trust in the listener/reader with the hope of empathy, forgiveness, compassion. It is burdensome knowledge that must be shared, it is also a tribute, because it is made to someone who has the power to understand and/or forgive. This is what a confession purports to be. It seemingly stems from a desire to reveal a morally vulnerable core as it simultaneously demands sympathy and even admiration, while it heroically performs its emotional striptease. And yet as readers we are often betrayed—the confession is not worthy of our attention. Wordsworth's stealing of the boat as a child ought not to qualify as a confession, Mitchell implies. And yet it is written and received as one. How does that happen?

Writing on autobiography, de Man says, 'autobiography is a not a genre or a mode, but a figure of reading or of understanding that occurs to some degree in all texts'[2] (920). This insight may be pertinently applied to confessional writing as well. The genre does not determine whether a work is a confession, instead it is perhaps constituted by signifiers that gesture towards a confession. A confession seems to get conveyed through a shared cultural understanding of particular signifiers.

In this paper I will look at Alice Munro's short fiction, which whether autobiographical or not, often carry the tone, the vocabulary, the emotions that gesture towards a confession. I would like to locate such moments in order to speculate on what constitutes her confessions. Are there points of similarity or difference? What do they seem to ask of the reader? Do they arise out of shame or guilt? Do they ask for understanding or admiration?

I will confine myself to an assortment of stories that employ the first person narrative, even though I don't think that is a necessary prerequisite for a confession. Yet there is something immediately seductive about the first person narrative that immediately signals the confessional urgency.

'Red Dress-1946' tells the story of a young girl's anxiety about her high school dance:

> But what was really going on in the school was not Business practice and Science and English, there was something else that gave life its urgency and brightness. That old building with its rock walled clammy basements and black cloakrooms and pictures of dead royalties and lost explorers, was full of the tension and excitement of sexual competition, and in this, in spite of daydreams of vast successes, I had premonitions of total defeat. Something had to happen, to keep me from total defeat .... (Red Dress, 151)[3]

The anxiety, the confiding manner, the urgent need to strike out, all signal towards the expectation of complete identification by her readers. The narrator's childhood, though far away, does not allow distance through irony. She has no possibility of avoiding this dread event that is going to test her, because her mother has painstakingly stitched her a red dress. Predictably, the evening flounders. She plans to escape her humiliation by running away with another girl who has not been asked out either. At that very moment she gets invited by a boy. Before she knows what's happening, she is dancing, performing her gender by the rule book. The narrator admits no gratification from this moment, only a sense of defeat. When 'I saw the waiting kitchen, and my mother in her faded, fuzzy kimono, with her sleepy but doggedly expectant face, I understood what a mysterious and oppressive obligation I had, to be happy, and how I had almost failed it, and would be likely to fail it, every time, and she would not know' (160).

The reader is invited to share this secret. Here's a confession of failure after the earlier premonition of utter defeat. But the narrator has had a degree of success. Then what constitutes the failure? Her partial relief is obscured by the knowledge of her complicity with a pattern she has found oppressive. And what is the real failure? Is it the failure of a girl who is almost ignored at the school dance, but gets asked just when she's about to run away? Is the failure of a daughter who fails to be happy despite her mother's efforts? Or is it a failure to live up to expectations of female solidarity when she lets down the other girl whom nobody wants to dance with? Perhaps all of these. Finally, it seems to me that the real defeat eludes definition. Instead what pervades the story is an overwhelming sense of defeat. There are repeated failures—shame at having been almost rejected by the boys, a shame at having let down the one girl who gave her solace and guilt at having let down her mother. The confusion about the nature of failure is perhaps linked with her contradictory desires of succeeding as a girl in conventional terms, on the one hand, and as someone who rejects the tyranny of mating rituals, on the other hand. It is this confusion that is passed on in the confession to a reader who shares a similar cultural understanding. What is asked of the reader? Is the earlier sexual anxiety really building a case for the later betrayal? It seems to me that Munro's narrator needs to justify her fragmented, unfaithful self to her imagined audience. It seems to me as if the confession of betrayal works here not just to expiate herself, but there is in fact a larger agenda of establishing desire as contradictory, conflicted and hence always elusive.

'Boys and Girls', written around the same time, looks at the construction of gender identity. The narrator here belongs to rural Ontario and talks about the rituals of fox farming with affection, with no trace of squeamishness. There is a deliberate engagement with masculine spaces that emphasize the narrator's distance from conventional femininity. Old horses need to be shot down in this space and the narrator sneaks a look with her little brother once and is only a little shaken. But when it is the turn of her own favourite old mare, she quietly leaves the gates open, for her to run away. This gets reported by her elder brother.

> Everybody at the table was looking at me. I nodded swallowing food with great difficulty. To my shame, tears flooded my eyes.
>
> My father made a curt sound of disgust. "What did you do that for"?
>
> I did not answer. I put down my fork and waited to be sent from the table, still not looking up.
>
> But this did not happen. For some time nobody said anything, then Laird said matter-of-factly, "She's crying."
>
> "Never mind," my father said. He spoke with resignation even good humour, the words which absolved and dismissed me for good. "She's only a girl," he said.
>
> I didn't protest that, even in my heart. Maybe it was true (171).

Obviously the narrator's humane act serves as a critique of gratuitous male violence embedded in masculine rituals. What is really the point here once again is the narrator's silence of complicity with the father who overlooks it as an act of female weakness. The real weakness then is in the way she allows the father to absolve and dismiss her. That is what constitutes the confession. The last line poses a problem. 'I didn't protest that, even in my heart'. Why does the narrator not protest—even in her heart? Had she remained silent but felt indignant, it would still have been a confession of weakness. By adding that her father may actually have been right, she questions more fundamentally the politics of gender. Is she trying retrospectively to justify her silence? The secret knowledge passed on to the reader is once again of complicity with the very patriarchy that she seeks to critique. The writer then assumes it will be read as a moment where she fails what is a fundamental faith of feminism. The gentle irony at her own expense, is a plea for forgiveness.

Earlier in the story she talks of daydreams and describes her fantasies:

> A story might start off in the old way, with a spectacular danger, a fire or wild animals, and for a while I might rescue people; then things

> would change around, and instead, somebody would be rescuing me. It might be a boy from our class at school, or even Mr. Campbell, our teacher, who tickled girls under the arms. And at this point the story concerned itself at great length with what I looked like—how long my hair was, and what kind of dress I had on; by the time I had these details worked out the real excitement of the story was lost. (127)

In her fantasies the narrator records her troubled self, unable to seek happiness—now as a conventional male hero, now as a conventional heroine. The fantasy breaks down in confusion as neither renouncing womanhood nor announcing it seem either convincing or satisfying. The confusion here clearly connects with an awareness of gender as a performance that remains embedded in a series of conventional gestures and must therefore fail to provide any real gratification. If we now return to the end, where she confessed her complicity with the father, her failure to inscribe herself, her capitulation to her father's act of dissolving her, it then seems to add to contradictory ways of understanding gender—either as fleeting performance or as being essentially inscribed and fixed—the freewheeling fantasies get challenged by the later closure. The earlier passage where she talks of her fantasies, is only an acknowledgement of an instability of gender constructions. This knowledge is necessary to understand the end as failure. Her tacit acquiescence to her father becomes a failure only because she has experienced the vulnerability of gender roles. Thus her failure may be understood once again as stemming from contradictory desires—to please her father, to be heroic, to have her way, to seem obedient. But what gets foregrounded here is the contradictory self which is fluid, temporal, incomplete and endlessly making itself through repeated re-writing. Confession here helps to enforce closure on a self subjected repeatedly to flux by its contradictory desires.

'The Office' departs from the stories discussed earlier because here Munro turns attention to writing. It begins with a woman who wants space to write and finally decides to rent an office. But her freedom is shortlived as the landlord inserts himself relentlessly. He tries to inveigle himself by telling her about the old tenant, hinting at sleazy secrets, inflicting unwanted presents. When she tries to shut him out, he turns vicious and finally forces her to leave. She imagines him at the end, 'sorrowfully arranging in his mind the bizarre but somehow never quite satisfactory narrative of yet another betrayal of trust. While I arrange words, and think it is my right to be rid of him' (74).

The last line once again becomes troubling. Till then it is a very predictable story about women being squeezed for space, denied freedom to write and even failure to find space. The way the landlord Mr Malley arranges stories is also commented upon, but the last line draws a parallel between the narrator and her persecutor. Both invent narratives—both are self-assured about the veracity of their truths. Is this story a confession? I would answer in the affirmative. Inasmuch as it admits to the act of writing as being only a version of truth, a biased version of truth, and the storyteller being blind to her biases, it works as a confession. Like most self-deprecatory comments, this one too expects admiration rather than judgement. Here then is a writer/narrator who, even as she arranges the truth, sees herself as doing so, and there ends the parallel between the neurotic landlord and her. The story then feels the need to insert a self-objectifying statement in an otherwise mundane search for space. How do we understand this need to ironically reflect on writing? As specific to women who need to reiterate their humility? As a necessary symptom of postmodernism? Why is it brought only at the end? Why is it so briefly dwelt on? Does it function like a twist in the tale? To me it seems as if the brief twist of irony rescues the story from being a classic tale of female persecution and the hint of self-reflexive irony allows the writer to distance herself from earlier narratives by women. The confession then helps create a privileged status for the writer through an ironic expression of an anxiety.

In a much later collection of stories, Munro reflects on writing again. Two of her stories, 'Family Furnishings' and

'Queenie' narrated in the first person actually are about people the narrator claims to have known closely, even intimately. If at all they talk about the self it is done incidentally.

'Family Furnishings' is the portrait of an aunt, the *enfant terrible* of the family. She is both a figure of scandal for the conservative, provincial family and simultaneously an immensely attractive figure. As the narrator recalls her childhood, she talks of how she would try to win the admiration of this one figure by talking irreverently. Later she grows into a writer and in hindsight, Alfrida, the glamorous aunt, appears sordid, even pathetic. 'Now that I was living in that city I seldom looked at ... that had once seemed to me... the centre of our life at home, sixty miles away. The jokes, the compulsive insincerity of people like Alfrida ... now struck me as tawdry and boring' (100–1).[4]

The roles are reversed as the aunt feels the rejection. Years later when the narrator meets Alfrida's biological daughter, she reported that, Alfrida said, 'you were a kind of a cold fish.' And 'she said you were smart, but you weren't ever quite as smart as you thought your were.' The wounding comments are met stonily, but later the narrator casually mentions, 'I did not think of the story I would make about Alfrida not of that in particular—but of the work I wanted to do, which seemed more like grabbing something out of the air than constructing stories' (119). Here is a confession about writing, about an unfeeling self and a writing self. The narrator endorses Alfrida's having called her a cold fish who will grab anything out of air to tell a story. Does she imply that all writing draws upon intimacies with others, that it infringes upon their lives and the distance with them comes from a self that is constantly shifting, slipping, becoming new? Does the need to confess stem from a desire to justify the writer who appropriates other lives because after it gets written, it seems to have nothing to do with them? She admits she understands the wearing out of old attachments in her own life, but sees it happen only in her own life? The writer of today has little to do with the person who had the experiences then, is what she seems to say. The apparent lack of guilt could actually be seen as a way of dealing with the self in flux, the self unwilling to remain fixed, a disorderly, fragmentary self.

'Queenie' is about the narrator's stepsister who culturally and socially represents very different values. yet she is like her alter-ego; she wears gaudy make up, elopes with a widower, sells cinema tickets, does not go to college, she recklessly desires to achieve social and sexual success, while the narrator is 'innocent 'of such desires'. It is an affectionate, wistful portrait, nevertheless even as it poignantly looks back at the time spent together, the narrator recognizes her desire to be entirely unreciprocated. Queenie eludes her, refuses to recognize or keep in touch, refuses to remain the same person, constantly reinvents herself. The narrator implies that she is the opposite: stable, consistent, concrete. The story could have ended with Queenie lost to the narrator, on the note of nostalgia that ripples through the narrative. But it doesn't. Instead she ends as under:

'But now something has happened ... I have a notion that sometimes I see Queenie. It's not through any particular wish or effort that I see her, and it's not as if I believe it is really her, either ... . I found myself going in one direction and then in one direction and then in another ... looking straight into people's faces, and probably frightening them, because I was silently beseeching them to tell me where I could find Queenie.

Until I come to my senses and convinced myself that it wasn't possible, and that whoever was or was not Queenie had left me behind' (274).

When the narrator confesses that she doesn't believe it's Queenie, it is an epiphanic moment which makes evident the fact that Queenie is really a part of her. She is not her stepsister, but a part of herself that she has left behind. If we re-examine the story now in the light of the recurrent anxiety in Munro, the anxiety of leaving behind selves and inventing selves that seem far away—we can read Queenie as addressing an anxiety about the self. How do we reconcile the slippery, elusive selves? Can we really write off the past selves? Is distance both inevitably painful and desirable? 'Queenie' examines the same territory as 'Family

Furnishings', but while 'Queenie' converts it into a nostalgic quest, 'Family Furnishings' denies nostalgia, insisting upon seeing reinvention as emancipatory, desirable and inevitable. How do we make sense of these changing moods? The urge to return seems to be compulsive. The different moods seem to suggest again the quest for the real emotion: What is the relationship with the past, childhood, memory? In trying to be faithful to herself, does Munro return to similar sites? Is she searching for the overarching truth? There is an inevitable discomfort in the process and she appears to repeat similar patterns of guilt and failure. What seems gratifying in her narratives is the desire to 'expose' herself. I would echo what Paul de Man says about Rousseau, his shame is real because he knows he commits the crimes in order to able to exhibit himself.

In the few stories discussed above, I have tried to isolate what I think is the common strain in Munro's narratives, to see what constitutes such moments. These moments almost always contain a shaping impulse, a desire to hold on and define the amorphousness of gender identity and the fragile constructions of the self, but the endings often seem to enforce a closure, to assert or conclude. Yet we see the same themes revisited, often with differing emphases, we see the compulsion to speak in the same voice. If we are then to understand meaning as constituted not just by the content or the conclusion, but through the contradictions and the repetitions, we would recognize the slippery terrain of the confession, haunted by different ghosts, steadily turning the gaze upon itself, and seizing hold of moments that promise certitude, but crumbling away under the lingering gaze of the reader to reveal the fleeting nature of such epiphanic insights. The mask slips, only to reveal, as the French philosopher Condillac once wrote, the costume beneath.

Endnotes

1. Jacques Derrida. "'A Madness' Must Watch Over Thinking" quoted in Joseph Kronick. Points ... Interviews', 1974–1994. ed. Elisabeth Weber. Trans. Peggy Kamuf and other (NY: Routledge, 1995). Joseph G. Kronick further writes "although Derrida admits to

responding to the lure of a speculative totality, his autobiography is a kind of shattering of the mirror in order to face the other to whom he is responsible. In its traditional sense, autobiography aims to make transparent to the writing self the life of the historical self" (998).

2. de Man, Paul, 'Autobiography as De-facement,' MLN.94: 919–30. 1979. 919–930
3. Munro, Alice. "Red Dress-1946". *Dance of the Happy Shades.* (London: Vintage, 2000) 147–160. Henceforward referred to as *Dance*, p. 151.
4. Munro, Alice. *Hateship, Friendship, Courtship, Loveship, Marriage,* (London: Vintage, 2001).

REFERENCES

de Man, Paul, 'Autobiography as De-facement,' MLN.94:919–30. 1979. 919–930

—, *Allegories of Reading: Figural Language in Rousseau, Nietzsche, Rilke and Proust,* New Haven and London, Yale University Press, 1979.

Foucault, Michel, *The History of Sexuality*: An introduction. Vol. 1, 1976. Trans. Robert Hurley, New York: Vintage Books, 1978

Kronick, Joseph G. "'A Madness' Must Watch Over Thinking" in Points ... Interviews', 1974–1994. Ed. Elisabeth Weber. trans. Peggy Kamuf et al. (New York: Routledge, 1995).

Mitchell, W.J.T. "Influence, Autobiography and Literary History: Rousseau's *Confessions* and Wordsworth's *The Prelude.*" ELH, 57: 614–64.1990

Munro, Alice, *Dance of the Happy Shades* (1968). London, Vintage. 2000.

—, *Hateship, Friendship, Courtship, Loveship, Marriage*. London. Vintage, 2001.

CHAPTER 14

The Role of Focalization in the Construction of the Self

A Study of Three Canadian Short Stories

Preeti Bhatt

Works of fiction construct the 'self' of the characters or the protagonist through description, dialogue, interior monologue and narration. A piece of narrative fiction gradually builds the self of the character, endowing it with depth and realistic attributes, and thereby evokes the reader's empathy with the characters. If the self of the character is vividly imagined and sensitively created by the writer through the narrative, the reader relates to the characters during the process of reading, and almost relives the experiences of the characters due to his/her empathy with them. The construction of the subjectivity of the characters is a delicate process, and much of the success of the narrative enterprise depends upon how poignantly the human dimension is attributed to the character by the writer. While experimental writers often interrogate the verisimilitude of the constructed world of the text by foregrounding the artifice of the narrative through self-reflexivity or unreliable narration, convincing characters have to be created in the narrative by them initially to put forward the proposition of the unreality of the narrated text.

The present paper seeks to examine the construction of the self or the subject in works of fiction through the process of focalization, i.e., the presentation of events or situations in fiction through the consciousness of one or more characters, or that of a detached narrator. Multiple meanings are generated and a complex self is created through variations in focalization in narrative works. This paper will focus on three Canadian short stories: Margaret Atwood's 'Bluebeard's Egg', George Bowering's 'The Creature', and Helen Weinzweig's 'My Mother's Luck'. A study of these short stories will allow one to understand how focalization negotiates the reader's response to the narrative and helps to create a multidimensional self of the subject.

This paper is divided into two sections. The first section initially discusses the portrayal of the nature of the self in literature and moves on to discuss the technique of focalization used by writers to create a complex, multilayered self of the characters in fiction. This section also briefly considers the theoretical premises relating to the use of focalization in literature. The second section attempts to relate the experimental narrative technique of these stories to their Canadian origins. It then moves on to analyse the technique of focalization as used in these stories to create the subjectivity of the characters.

I

In works of literature, the self is portrayed in innumerable ways, and the complex nature of the self is explored through its conflict with society or due to its innate contradictions. Jonathan Culler in the *Literary Theory* (1997) discusses two basic premises which influence modern thinking about the self of the subject. Culler asks, 'Is the self something *given* or something *made*, and, second, should it be conceived in *individual* or in *social* terms?' (108) The combinations of these two categories generate four contrasting views about the creation of the self—the self as something unique; as formed as a product of its origins and social attributes; as something changeable; and as a subject position it occupies.

The question of what constitutes the self of the subject is one of the foremost preoccupations of literature. Most works of fiction use either of these attributes of the self as the focal point which the text explores. The self is seen to be a cumulative outcome of the combination of its past, the choices it makes and the impact of social forces upon it. The conflict experienced by an individual in society and as portrayed in literature also originates from the opposition between these four positions occupied by the self as enumerated above.

However, how the self is constituted in any work of fiction depends upon the perspective from which it is represented. Culler points out, 'Discussions of narrative frequently speak of the 'point of view from which a story is told', but this use of *point of view* confuses two separate questions: who speaks? and whose vision is presented?' (88). The narrator whose voice is projected through the story may be distinct from the character whose vision is presented in the narrative. The perceptive reader needs to make a distinction between these two perspectives.

The term 'focalization', developed by such theorists as Gerard Genette and Mieke Bal, indicates the consciousness or position through which events in the narrative are presented to the reader. The narrator, therefore, may or may not overlap with the focalizer of events in the story. The question 'who speaks' then becomes separate from 'who sees'. The 'narrative voice', or the voice of the narrative discourse which establishes a communicative contact with the reader (Genette, 186) may be distinguished from the focalizer. John Manfred defines the focalizer as 'the agent whose point of view orients the narrative text' (*Narratology*, N3.2.2) while Genette describes focalization as the 'different points of view from which … the action is looked at' (161). Modifying Genette's term, Rimmon–Kenan introduced the term 'external focalizer' for the focalizer who is external to the story, also called narrator—focalizer, as the focus of perception appears to be that of the narrator (74). An 'internal focalizer' is a focus of perception of a character in the story, also called the character—focalizer. Focalization thus becomes a means of anchoring a person's point of view to present his/her thoughts, reflections and understanding, the true or imaginary perceptions, and the cultural or ideological position of that person in the narrative.

The variations in focalization influence the overall effect of the narrative. While an omniscient narrator may give an impression of the comprehensibility of the world, the limited point of view of a single character, called 'a figural narrative situation' by Franz K. Stanzel (184–85), offers a unidimensional view of the self of the protagonist. The restricted point of view of a single protagonist foregrounds the unpredictability of all events and situations. Stories which juxtapose multiple points of view allow the reader a more objective understanding of the characters and events portrayed. Contemporary works of fiction experiment with focalization to create complex subjects or selves in the narrative.

II

The three Canadian short stories being analysed in this paper are experimental in form and employ the technique of focalization imaginatively to create the self of the characters—selves, which embody the contradictions, the enigmas, the *angst* of real human beings. In the introduction to the anthology of Canadian short stories from which these stories have been taken, Manorama Trikha puts up the question, 'Is there anything distinctly Canadian about Canadian short stories?' (9). While examining these short stories, one is forced to ponder over the relationship between the striking element of postmodernist experimentation in these stories and their Canadian origins. Shirin Kudchedkar in *Postmodernism and Feminism* points out that 'the strategies of postmodernism allow Canadian writers to bring in the context. Explanations for this are variously found in the heterogeneity of the Canadian experience, the Canadian self as a "hyphenated" self and Canada's postcolonial situation' (19). The provisional, pluralistic Canadian identity with its multicultural influences and its colonialist past finds expression in the postmodern techniques of fragmentation, ambiguity and contradiction of these stories. Jancy James also finds a similarity between the postmodernist impulse and the sense of Canadianness. She states that if postmodernism signifies 'the urge to transform, manipulate and if possible, subvert the native and acquired legacies ... the Canadian situation being a postcolonialist cultural and political phenomenon, characteristically reflects the postmodernist response to reality' (100). The varying uses of focalization in these stories thus help to build the Canadian self with its multilayered sense of reality/existence.

In order to examine the shaping of the self of the protagonist through varying narratorial perspectives, I now move on to discuss three stories by Atwood, Bowering and Weinzweig. The first story which I take up for analysis is Margaret Atwood's 'Bluebeard's Egg' published in 1983. The story is presented from a third-person point of view and is focalized through the character of Sally. Using the term coined by Genette, it is a 'heterodiegetic' narrative, where the story is told by a narrator who is *not* present as a character in the story. While explaining this term, Genette states, 'We will therefore distinguish here two types of narrative: one with the narrator absent from the story he tells [...], the other with the narrator present as a character in the story he tells [...]. I call the first type, ... *heterodiegetic*, and the second type *homodiegetic*' (244–45). To quote the incipient of Atwood's story, 'Sally stands at the kitchen window, waiting for the sauce she's reducing to come to a simmer, looking out' (45). Here, the narrator employed is a 'covert' one, a term suggested by Seymour Chatman in *Story and Discourse* (1978), where he points out that 'in covert narration we hear a voice speaking of events, characters and setting, but its owner remains hidden in the discoursive shadows'. Chatman goes on to explain that in a covertly narrated story, 'one can express a character's speech or thoughts in indirect form' (197). In Atwood's story the narrator withdraws behind the protagonist whom the reader encounters in the first word of the story. The entire narrative is presented from Sally's point of view—her thoughts, memories, and also her actions are described using the third person 'she' by the narrator. This is a typical figural narrative situation wherein the heterodiegetic narrator tries to reproduce Sally's impressions in an internal focalization. And yet, her innermost perceptions are presented by the narrator with such accuracy that the reader presumes that the character Sally and the narrator are one.

A single narrative situation—the dinner which Sally has organized for her husband Ed's cardiologist friends, forms the focus of the story. The story describes the events as perceived by Sally from the noon to the night on the same day, and gradually opens the whole subjective landscape of her consciousness. As the narrative progresses, the complex dilemmas which torment Sally gradually unfold.

Sally, married to a successful and attractive heart specialist, is assailed by a nagging feeling of insecurity for her married life. This fear is not unfounded, for Sally is the third wife of Ed, and has no inkling of why the earlier two wives left him. The narrator states, 'His protestations of ignorance, his refusal to discuss the finer points, is frustrating to Sally ... But it's also cause for anxiety; if he doesn't know what happened to the other two, may be the same thing could be happening with her and he doesn't know about that either' (47). As Ed is a cardiologist, women tend to flock around him, both those who are genuinely heart patients, and those who are not, 'everywhere he goes he is beset by sirens. They want him to fix their hearts' (50). Sally can only observe with increasing anxiety and trepidation the flirtatious encounters of these women with her husband.

Parallel to Sally's experiential reality is the folktale of Bluebeard's Egg—a story which her teacher Bertha of the evening course on the 'Forms of Narrative Fiction' has asked her to rewrite in the realistic mode. This folk tale, recreating the domination of the patriarchal order is about a wizard in disguise as he allures three sisters one by one to his majestic house in the forest, entrusting each of them with an egg and a key to a room which they are forbidden to enter. The first two sisters unwittingly meet their death when they open the room, and find inside 'a large basin of blood, within which were the bodies of many women, which had been cut to pieces; nearby was a chopping block and an axe' (63). Horrified by what they have seen, they drop the egg with fear into the basin, which becomes stained with blood, and when the wizard sees the bloodstain, he chops them into pieces and throws their bodies too into the basin. The third sister unlocks the door with the key but does not carry the egg inside the forbidden room. When she discovers her dead sisters inside, she joins their body parts again, which brings them to life, and thus causes the wizard to lose his power over them.

Point of view acquires importance in Atwood's story as Sally ponders over the question of whose point of view should she write the story of Bluebeard's egg from. She thinks of the forbidden room and the chopped-up women, then thinks of the egg as the fertility symbol, and decides to write the story from the egg's point of view. She wonders, 'But how can there be a story from the egg's point of view, if the egg is so closed and unaware?' (65) Soon Sally inadvertently sees Ed and her close friend Marilyn in a position of physical compromise which suggests that their relationship is more complex and deeper than it appears. Her fears of her marriage threaten to come true and the egg acquires a living shape in her mind: 'But now she's seeing the egg, which is not small and cold and white and inert but larger than a real egg and golden pink … . Its almost pulsing; Sally is afraid of it' (70). As Sally thinks of the egg as alive and about to hatch, the egg becomes the pivot of the whole story both of the folktale and of Sally wherein reality is hidden deep inside the core, and the surface reality is only misleading.

In the story the narrator is covert and the text projects a sense of directness and immediacy and the readers are drawn into the story experiencing themselves to be co-participants in the story. It places the narrator in the background and foregrounds internal focalization of the protagonist Sally. The main objective of internal focalization in this story is to attract attention to the mind of the focalizer Sally, away from the covert narrator and from the process of narratorial mediation.

The covert narrator in 'Bluebeard's Egg' also serves a stylistic purpose, of distancing the self-reflexive element of the story. The reader gradually realizes that the structure and motif of the folktale of Bluebeard's Egg is replicated in Atwood's story about Sally. So while Sally writes a transposition of the folktale of Bluebeard in the realistic mode, fairy-tale motifs are conspicuously present in her own story—Sally is the third wife of Ed (like the third sister), who unwittingly places trust in her husband and sees his stupidity as innocence, lamblike (46) until the truth spills out (as in the folktale), the repeated reference to the sauce she is cooking for the party, Ed as a heartman, other women as sirens, who, Sally tells Ed, 'think, you are delicious. They'll gobble you up. They'll chew you into tiny pieces' (57). The resonances in both the stories are so similar that the reader realizes that Sally's story which he/she has in hand is the modern realistic version of the folktale of Bluebeard's Egg. Consequently, the ontological status of Sally becomes dubious—is she a real human being, or in Barthes' words, a 'paper' woman, who in turn, is writing about another Sally, and so on. Mieke Bal in 'Notes on Narrative Embedding' refers to such stories within stories wherein, the original narrative becomes a 'frame' or 'matrix' narrative, and the story told by the narrating character becomes an 'embedded' or 'hyponarrative' (43). Atwood's narrative becomes an exemplary postmodernist text—a *mise-en-abyme*—due to the Chinese-box effect of a story within a story and that again within another, i.e., an endless succession of internal duplications. The subtle internal focalization of Sally, the protagonist, delays the reader's discovery of the metafictional nature of Atwood's narrative.

Variations in focalization in George Bowering's 'The Creature' serve to construct the complex self of the protagonist of the story. Here the narrative alternates between a third-person point of view which occurs in regular print, and first-person narration which appears in italicized print. The third-person narration which forms a major part of the narrative suggests a mental disorder, a paralysing phobia of death in the protagonist's mind. This phobia, the reader discovers, had its root back in time, for he witnessed the suicide of a young couple when he was ten years old. The fear he experiences is so strong that it is attributed the shape of a creature in the narrative, 'He probably stank, the creature stank of foul long-dead flesh and strained minerals and the torture of steel' (99). The third-person narrative is highly metaphorical and unrealistic in its description of the unnamed protagonist's paranoia. And yet, it is not a subconscious anxiety, for other characters are shown to be aware of the protagonist's obsession with death.

In the italicized passages, the first person narrator deliberately 'writes about life' (105). He describes in detail his experience of watching the birth of his daughter, who, presumably, is his nineteen year old daughter in the third person descriptions. The italicized first person passages are vivacious and true to life in their expression of the father's exuberance and excitement as his daughter is born. And yet these passages can be taken to be a fictional projection of himself, for the covert narrator states in the third person narrative that 'he knew that all writing was incorrect. Decent but incorrect' (99). The passages written in the autobiographical mode apparently represent a conscious endeavour on the part of the protagonist to negate 'the clinical depression' from which he suffers (101). The act of writing thus becomes an act of recreating life. Simultaneously, however, the entire fictional world projected in Bowering's story becomes unstable and dubious in the light of this interpretation.

In Helen Weinzweig's 'My Mother's Luck' published in 1989, the narrative is in the form of an unmarked quotation of the speech of the mother Lily, as she is about to send her daughter Esther to her estranged father Isaac, who is now divorced from Lily. The story opens with the line, 'I have decided, my mother said, to go with you to New York to see you off. Your boat sails a week from tomorrow. In a week you will be gone; who knows if we will ever see each other again' (119). What follows is a long first person narrative discourse, within which are described Lily's experiences as she tried to make both ends meet with her job of marcelling at a beauty parlour, her three unsuccessful marriages, the desperate measures she resorted to in order to get a divorce, the rearing of her daughter, Esther, from her first marriage in such troubled circumstances, and her gradual realization that, 'Each time I think, this time it will be different, but every man is your father all over again, in a fresh disguise. Talk. Talk. How could they talk' (122). Yet there are no reporting clauses in the passage except the initial one, and if that is overlooked, one would not realize that the entire story is being told by the daughter to an unspecified audience. The daughter's opening words, 'My mother said', form the frame narrative, and the mother's speech in the first person forms the embedded narrative.

Lily refers time and again to her sore feet, aching due to standing and working all day in the beauty parlour. These references occur like a refrain which repeatedly brings the temporal plane of the narrative from the distant past to the immediate present. Lily complains, 'All I have from life is sore feet. My poor feet, look how calloused and shapeless they have become. Once I had such fine hands and feet. The ankles, they used to be so thin' (122). The first person narration builds the persona of the mother, yet the fact cannot be ignored that it has been mediated through the consciousness of the daughter. The reader has to discount the changes which might have been caused by the impression of time, memory and personal prejudices of the daughter upon the original parting words of the mother. Similarly, while the discourse of the mother is an autobiographical utterance, and poignant though it is, the reader cannot ascertain whether it is the absolute truth or what she describes as her past, has been distorted by the human tendency to gloss over personal weaknesses, to present oneself as a victim of circumstances, of others, of hard luck. The narrative ends on the same note, without clearly indicating that the daughter's speech has come to an end, 'It's one o'clock already! Let's go to bed ... Remember, never leave dirty dishes around. Show your father I brought you up right ... Just think, in a week you will be on the ocean ... I'll turn out the light' (130).

Each of these three narratives is postmodernist in its approach to reality, its plurality of perspectives and the element of ontological rupture; highlighting a break with 'traditional genre boundaries and narrative patterns' (Kudchedkar, 179). Linda Hutcheon in *The Canadian Postmodern* also draws attention to the regionalist element in Canadian narratives, its 'concern for the different, the local, the particular—in opposition to the uniform, the universal, the centralized' (19). This *ex*-centricity is foregrounded through the splitting of the narrative voice, its fragmentation, and its refusal to admit a single vision in these narratives. The closed, unified subject in these Canadian stories is opened to an expression of multiplicity of voices, of subjectivities, of ontological levels through the use of focalization.

The conscious play with focalization in these three short stories constructs the complex selves of the subjects and simultaneously deconstructs them. While the characters are attributed multidimensional contours by providing intricate details about their mental processes, their social milieu, their past experiences, the subversion of meaning is achieved by the experimental use of focalization. Through narratives focalized, through multiple perspectives, the writers, Atwood, Bowering and Weinzweig successfully evoke questions in the reader's mind about the nature of the self, and the role of imagination and point of view in any narrative discourse.

REFERENCES

Atwood, Margaret. 'Bluebeard's Egg'. *Canadian Short Stories*. ed. Manorama Trikha. 45–70.

Bal, Mieke. 1978. 'Notes on Narrative Embedding'. *Poetics Today* 2.2 (1981): 41–59.

Bowering, George. 'The Creature'. *Canadian Short Stories*. ed. Manorama Trikha. 99–106.

Chatman, Seymour. *Story and Discourse: Narrative Structure in Film and Fiction*. New York: Cornell University Press, 1978.

Culler, Jonathan. *Literary Theory: A Very Short Introduction*. Oxford: Oxford University Press, 1997.

Genette, Gerard. *Narrative Discourse: An Essay in Method*. 1972. Trans. Jane E. Lewin. Ithaca: Cornell University Press, 1980.

James, Jancy. 'Canadian Paradigms of Postmodern Feminism.' *Postmodernism and Feminism: Canadian Contexts*. Ed. Shirin Kudchedkar. 99–111.

Kudchedkar, Shirin, ed. *Postmodernism and Feminism: Canadian Contexts*. Delhi: Pencraft International, 1995.

Narratology: A Guide to the Theory of Narrative. Ed. John Manfred. 28 May 2005. 15 May 2008. <http://www.uni.koeln.de/~amco2/pppn.htm.>

Rimmon–Kenan, Shlomith. *Narrative Fiction: Contemporary Poetics*. London: Methuen, 1983.

Stanzel, Franz K. *A Theory of Narrative*. trans. Charlotte Goedsche. 1979. Cambridge: Cambridge University Press, 1984.

Trikha, Manorama. Introduction. *Canadian Short Stories*. ed. Manorama Trikha. 9–13.

—, ed. *Canadian Short Stories*. Delhi: Pencraft International, 1993.

Weinzweig, Helen. 'My Mother's Luck'. *Canadian Short Stories*. Ed. Manorama Trikha. 119–130.

CHAPTER 15

A Narrative of Self-Reclamation

Ramabai Espinet's *The Swinging Bridge*

Charu Mathur

All writing is rooted in experience and felt reality and is often a filtered expression of the writer's 'self'. The 'self' however is a surprisingly elusive idea, intuitively obvious to commonsense, yet notoriously evasive to definition. For, what after all, is the 'self' that the self-narratives are supposed to be about? Is it that there is some essential 'self' within, that the writer needs to put into words? And, what function does that self-telling serve? Since, much of the writer's 'self' is inclusive of the unconscious and the subconscious that is concealed or distorted by conscious probing, writing can be a way of interacting with memories and experiences to overcome our resistance towards self-discovery. But, individuals constantly construct, deconstruct and reconstruct a 'self' to cope with needs and situations they encounter. The process of self-discovery is, therefore, an ongoing one in which the memories of the past and hopes and fears for the future play a vital role. Self-narratives are markers in the stages of a writers search for 'self' and are expressions of an accomplished, yet ironically, unfinished enterprise.

The Indo-Caribbean-Canadian writer, Ramabai Espinet's powerful yet lyrical first novel *The Swinging Bridge* maps such a journey towards self-discovery. Born in 1948 she grew up in San Fernando on the Caribbean island of Trinidad and was later displaced across the seas when her family immigrated to Canada in 1960. Her Indian roots can be traced back to the arrival of her ancestors from India to the island as indentured labour. Mona Singh, the protagonist and narrator of the novel traverses a similar historical, spatial and emotional journey from India to Trinidad, and then to Canada in an attempt to come to terms with her existence. The situational parallel between the writer and her creation crystallizes into a shared perspective of a culturally displaced woman trying to balance ideas of identity and home. This is not to say that Mona's story, in the novel, is Espinet's life story too, but that the novel is a site of common exploration and attempts to capture the dynamic and fluid qualities of the writer's 'self'-construction. 'Transference of experience or an imagined reality to the page', according to Jasbir Jain, 'involves a human agency rooted in inherited structures often internalized through socialization' (362). Indeed, the novel *The Swinging Bridge* is Espinet's attempt to come to terms with her social and cultural inheritance while embarking upon a journey of self-reclamation and redefinition. The protagonist Mona's profession of making documentaries about immigrant life in Canada is a way of recreating the predicament of her diasporic existence in Montreal. Her dream of 'going back and making films in her own place, on her own terms' is an expression of Espinet's search for her 'self' riding the vehicle of creativity (7). The novel voices the author's reconciliation with a painful historical past and embodies a collective rebirth of an uprooted and scattered generation.

The event that precipitates this literal and figurative journey is the impending death of Mona's forty-four year old brother Kello, who requests that she return to Trinidad to repurchase the family property that her father had sold several decades ago to move beyond his country roots in pursuit of 'an illusion of a better life' (25). Mona's encounter with family members in Trinidad and Toronto and her delving into boxes of memorabilia in both locations provide a natural framework for Espinet to locate herself within the complex matrix of family relationships and Indo-Trinidadian history. Through a first person narrative she reconstructs Mona's family saga and embarks upon a project of self-making in a way that memory and fiction mingle to strike at a deeper chord of experience.

Memory transports Mona to recall the various incidents of racial bias and cultural stereotypes she encounters while growing up in Trinidad. They had to submit to the prejudiced behaviour, or, as the man on the train told her, 'go back to where you came from' (45). The narrative draws the mindscape of the region and its impact on a growing child. Till 1970's when Espinet's family, like that of Mona, in the novel, migrated to Canada, the mainstream Trinidadian society was characterized by an Afro-Creole mode of existence, a world view that evolved out of the melting of African and European elements, which held all things Indian to be beneath the bar of a 'respectable' society. Since acts of 'self'-making are typically guided by unspoken, implicit cultural models of what selfhood should be, 'the racism of this place', as Mona exclaims, 'was always ready to crack you across your back when you least expected it' (35). Her crippled self-worth and a hostile relationship with her place of birth distorted her understanding of nationhood, trapped as they were 'by this perception of ourselves which is lodged in the hearts and minds of our fellow countrymen of other races' (70).

From early childhood, Mona was consumed by the thought of escape and dreamed of escaping with a gypsy caravan. But then, 'most people wanted some kind of escape from the place they lived, from their ordinary lives', and therefore, in spite of the 'big row', Da-Da sold their house and land to move to Canada (17). Colonization brought with it all the inherent prejudices and attitudes that shaped people to look outwards and direct their gaze to the white European for definition. It firmly established Europe as the source of all fantasy and the apex of all reality. Such are the vagaries of the empire that the narrator and her family, ultimately find themselves scattered across Canada, part of an Indian exodus, a flight of 'coolies' who have been marginalized by their 'creole' or African countrymen. However, ironically they discover even in their second migration walls and fences scrawled with graffiti that read 'Keep Canada White', and an ingrained, white-gloved racism so deep that people don't even know they are doing it (*The Swinging Bridge*: 237). 'All it took then in Trinidad', recounts Mona, 'was looking Indian, all it took now in Canada was skin colour. We had not moved one inch' (78).

They had simply shifted to a new land with old problems. Pitching around from one place to another had turned Mona into a 'nowarian' (147). She had always resisted anchorage, not wishing to be strangled by the disenfranchising constraints and conventions of her patriarchal Indian and Presbyterian community. 'I sometimes found myself entertaining the fancy of walking away from my flat', she confesses, 'leaving it open and ready for whatever chance occupant fate might send its way. A homeless person would be walking into an ordered shelter while I would be walking away' (147). Mona could never really understand Kello and Pappy's attachment to land, for 'ownership meant nothing to me', she says (53). Unable to define herself in terms of possession and belonging, she prefers to drift.

The defiance of roots leads to a bitterness of exile from one's own self. Inhabiting the outer margins of mainstream society it is no surprise that the dilemma of the visible minority whether in the Caribbean or in Canada has always been the construction of identity. According to Gillan, the plural is necessary not primarily because of the presence of different races/ethnicities that can govern identity, but because of the prismatic lens that colonialism has invented. Severe 'classism' were borne out of colourism and deeply embedded racism, economic and political dependency syndromes and an outward orientation where the Euro-American metropole was the standard and the subject, and the colonized lands the object ('West Indians are ignorant, frightened and ashamed of the past').

This gives rise to a suppressed desire to strike a blow of emancipation against the empire. 'The day is coming', wrote Da-Da in a letter to the editor, 'when right-thinking citizens like myself will not want their children to grow up in this country' (73). He was full of Indian pride when it suited him, an ancestral legacy that survived in many ways but is ignored and dismissed in reverence for the civilization of the colonizers. 'It was a time' Mona recalls, 'when newly educated people would throw out almost everything Indian at first, and would slowly gather back into their lives only those relics that were essential for survival' (28). Ambiguent positions like these made Espinet become conscious of the level of performance that operates in the public sphere, while the private sphere of home and family was a guarded domain.

One of the relics of the Indian cultural milieu that was preserved, was the formation of gender identities that reinforced the submissive model of womanhood. Women of colour faced a double negative by being both black and female. Mona's father encouraged her to become a scientist because it was an 'ideal profession' for her as she 'would be hidden from everyday contact with the world; pottering around in a hidden lab, emerging on occasion to astound the world with a remarkable discovery, then retreating to safety again' (172). Besides, gender prejudice was not divorced from racial discrimination. Mona's school teacher Miss Lee found her sexual curiosity predictable and deplorable: 'there was talk about how Indian girls were hot hot from small—no wonder they had to marry them off as children, and no wonder wife beating and chopping was common among these people' (140). Mona has difficulty in reconciling to the ways in which the mythical dimension of her Indianness constrains her. Also a victim of child abuse by uncle Baddall, the thought of marriage and domestic life filled her with irrational feelings of dread. She even resists commitment to her journalist lover Roddy and ends up losing him. Her need to be free was of paramount importance. 'My whole life' she declares, 'arches backwards and forwards according to the speed of the gust around me. In the centre, near the eye, in the place I live, it is still. A small mercy' (5). Her exploratory and transgressive 'self' was an inevitable consequence of the transitional space she inhabited.

Therefore, no matter how private the process of 'self'-making may be, it is always constructed by the tools and institutions of culture and history that act as invisible forces constituting the collective consciousness. In order to confront this elusive 'self', it is imperative to confront the unaddressed layers of the past. In the novel, Mona unearths the story of her great grandmother, Gainder, the unwanted Indian widow, a *rand* who came as an indentured labourer and began her mother's family (268). The hazardous and heart-wrenching crossing of the 'black waters', the *kala pani*, testifies to her enduring strength and becomes a symbol of the birth passage as the locus of all creation. It is a place of trauma with the promise of joyous birth and survival. Gainder had nothing when she arrived in Trinidad, but survived and so did her offspring. Mona's mother, however, had kept secret her lineage in favour of the preferred myth amongst Trinidadian Indians that an entire family and entirely respectable family had migrated. Besides, Grandma Lil's concealing snippets from her mother's life in shop books reveals the severe social compulsion of disassociation with their disreputable past and a fear of addressing its many legacies. Identities get constructed upon cultivated ignorance and distortions that lead to a sense of shame—both at the loss of history and the nature of distorted history.

This self-mortifying position renders the West Indian vulnerable. In an attempt to erase the past, many Indians in Trinidad became Christian converts while others resorted to allegiance to the church schools set up by Presbyterian missionaries from Canada as an adaptive measure to cope with the changed situation. These 'church people from Canada' interfered 'too much' in the lives of otherwise 'big strong men' in Trinidad (62). Unlike Christian marriages they did not recognize Hindu and Muslim marriages. Probing the past revealed how Mona's paternal grandfather Pappy, like her maternal grandmother Lil, too, had secrets tucked up his sleeves. He had a 'bamboo wife', Etwaria faithfully and patiently waiting for him (61). This was a truth of his life that he was pressurized by the church to ignore the earlier marriage in order to marry Mona's grandmother. Suspended between her legitimate and illegitimate lineage, there is an ambiguity that envelops Mona's sense of selfhood. It is only when she frees herself from social and moral concerns that her divided and unsituated selfhood feels grounded.

The novel begins by affirming Mona's escape into independence and autonomy, only to plunge her without warning back into the clutches of her past. Her openness to experimentation leads to a seemingly fulfilled 'self' but as she matures her lack of belonging begins to disturb her. Her careless abandon was born out of amnesia. And 'amnesia' according to Walcott, 'is the true history of the New World' (40). But since imposed forgetting cannot be a solution, confrontation with the ghosts of the past can be the only way to rid oneself of them. The pull of the 'navel strings' she realizes, is too strong to be ignored (75). Visiting the past becomes an exercise in forgiving and forgetting that leads to a reinvented 'self'. This 'self' seeks a reconciliation with troubled family relationships. Mona could now forgive her father for humiliating her by making her 'kneel down and walk across the yard cutting up [her] knees on the gravel' for wearing a 'shift dress' he disapproved of (203). Similarly, though her mother never tried to woo and win her love, she realized that her mother's signature was written on her life. 'Escape was my goal' she admits, 'the means, her eloquent gift to me' (214). Assisting the reclamation of their ancestral land in San Fernando symbolically signified an end of her drifting lifestyle. Running away from family history could no longer provide the required insulation. 'Something had cracked inside me' she feels, 'I feared that my shell would dissolve leaving me naked, bare for the entire world to see' (236). Her ability to face and reveal her true 'self' became her strength. For though it is important to have a sense of where you came from, that should not overshadow where you are. And therefore, back in Montreal, she is at peace with her own 'self'. 'I am part of this city I live in' she finally claims, 'and right now I want no other place. Like any other migrant navigating new terrain, I bring my own beat to the land around me' (300). Surrendering to the past had brought redemption and renewal.

The title of the novel *The Swinging Bridge* is a reference to the various bridges in the novel, all of them providing an insecure footing. Picked up from an incident in Mona's childhood when she experiences a moment of extreme peril on a suspension bridge, it foregrounds the role of another physical bridge—the gangplank on which the indentured women ascend into a ship that brings them to the Caribbean island. The metaphor refers to the uncertainty of the terrain on which these migrants and their future generations find themselves on. This uncertainty is part of her 'self' construction. Like her victory on the suspension bridge, she can triumph over her unanchored self by looking at history as a foundation for a new beginning. The 'New World', as Walcott puts it, 'does not pretend ... innocence, its vision is not naïve ... the apples of its second Eden have the tartness of experience' (41).

Espinet's articulation of her 'self', through the protagonist Mona, was a way of 'othering' the 'self'. The 'other' constitutes a position of outsidedness needed to complete the 'self'. Her contemplation of a person who is situated outside herself makes her more accessible to her own gaze. This position of advantage constructs a sense of ourselves by appropriating the position of the 'other', outside the 'self'. Writing the 'other' facilitates an understanding of the 'self'. Expressing herself through Mona, made Mona the author of Espinet's 'self'. The subjective being objectified she was able to dispassionately address the multiple dimensions of her past to arrive at a more comforting present.

REFERENCES

Espinet, Ramabai. *The Swinging Bridge*. New Delhi: Penguin, 2004.

Jain, Jasbir. "From Experience to Aesthetics: The Dialectics of Language and Representation", *Growing up as a Woman Writer*. Ed. Jasbir Jain. New Delhi: Sahitya Academy, 2007.

Walcott, Derek. "The Muse of History", *Critics on Caribbean Literature*. Ed. Edward Baugh. London: George Allen & Unwin, 1978.

Online

Gillan, Ayanna. "West Indians are ignorant, frightened and ashamed of their past", 20 Jan.2005 www.rootswomen.com/ayanna/articles/20012005. html. 3 May 2008.

CHAPTER 16

Interrogating the Arab-American Experience

The Novels of Diana Abu-Jaber

Nidhi Singh

The Arab-American literary tradition is traced back to 19th century and the credit for popularizing it in America is given to Kahlil Gibran. The spiritual quest for self in his works finds an echo in the immigrant experience. Gibran in *Sand and Foam* says: Only once have I been made mute. It was when a man asked me 'who are you?' (2)

These lines also voice the dilemma of the Arab-American writer struggling to break the silence to constitute an identity and the problematics of the act of writing the self. Elimaz Abinader in the article, 'Children of Al Mahjar: Arab-American Literature Spans a Century', informs that 'Literature by Arab-American writers is part of the syllabi of classes on ethnic literature, literature of immigration and multicultural voices'. In spite of the growing visibility now, Arab-American literature had not enjoyed similar popularity in the past.

Critics like Elimaz and Maryemma are of the view that the resurgence of Black American voice in the late 1960s led to the demand for space in American history and literature by other multicultural groups too. It is in the 1970s that with the upsurge of ethnic literature in America that Arab-American literature also registered its presence. The driving impulse, i.e., the need to define oneself to prevent being defined by others, seen behind the works produced by Arabs in America is shared by other marginalized immigrant communities too. The usage of 'others' here is intentional. The stereotyping of the marginalized groups is not confined to the literature produced by the mainstream. The marginalized too create stereotypes not only of the empowered centre, but also of other marginalized groups. The mutual othering at both the levels leads to isolation arising from an exclusionist approach, encouraging ghettoization. Uma Parmeswaran in 'Dispelling the Spells of Memory' refers to the impulse towards ghettoization inherent in the diasporic situation and says, 'Ghettoization comes from two sources-from within and from without the diasporic community. Once the numbers of any particular ethnic group increases, there seems to be a bigger move towards self-ghettoization … . Both exile and home are here, within the new home land' (318).

The dilemma of the writer with 'hyphenated' sensibility is the danger of either being sucked into the dominant literary trends by compromising the ethnic identity, or becoming confined to a system of expression that is at odds with the place and period to which it has been transported and transplanted. The 'golden mean' remains a mirage which the immigrant writers constantly aspire for.

Immigrant communities have to invariably face hostility in the country of adoption. Arabs in America too experience the rejection and marginalization based on race and religion. The cultural differences rooted in language, food, clothes, festivals—the very way of life, emphasizes 'difference' as strongly as the colour of their skin. In the post 9/11 global scenario when relations between America and Arab countries are marked by antagonism and an atmosphere of mutual distrust, the Arab-American writers face even more acutely the challenge of not only creating a space for literature produced by them, but also of self-definition.

The Arab immigration to America which is traced back to 1860s, continues. The causes remain the same: political oppression at home, economic considerations or a combination of both. The decades of violence, be it oppressive Ottoman regime persecuting Maronite Christians of Greater Syria in the 1860s or the incessant Palestine-Israel conflict, Arab-Israel War (1948), Iran-Iraq Gulf War (1980–88), Lebanon Civil War (1975–1990), Yemen Civil War (1962–1970) or even the ferment visible in present scenario, have made several Middle Easterners opt for America in their search for peace and personal advancement.

The first wave of immigrants to America, like diasporas world-wide, were oriented towards homeland. They were devoted to the land left behind and nostalgically remembered it as 'home' or 'old country'. There was an acute sense of alienation as they struggled to acclimatize themselves not only to the unfriendly climatic condition and geographic location, but also to alien language and culture. Inclined to oral rendition rather than the written, the few educated Arabs, amongst mostly poor and uneducated first wave Arab immigrants during late 19th century, took it upon themselves to publish journals and newspapers dealing with the Arab experience. These publications provided the foundation for the Arab-American literature.

The second wave of post-world war immigration consisted largely of educated Arabs. 1940s experienced a lull in literary output, but with the Civil Rights Movement followed by the Black Power Movement. New spaces for ethnic and marginalized voices were created not only for Afro-Americans, as pointed out by Maryemma Graham in 'Introduction' to *The African American Novel,* but also for other marginalized groups like Jewish-Americans, Arab-Americans. The emergence of Arab-American literature saw the rise of writers, who while they deal with the immigrant experience, also attempt to use the tension inherent in the situation for creative output. Reconstituting the identity in keeping with the demands of the new reality emerges as an increasingly contested site. A pressing need to define the Arab-American identity and to inscribe the Arab-American experience acutely was felt. The Arab-American writers wanted to write themselves into the literary history of America—*to write*, with a view to preventing to being written about. Contemporary writers are experimenting and exploring new areas as the dialectics of margins and the centre is being interrogated and they attempt to break free of the scaffolding of ethnic identity by rejecting the restrictive label of 'ethnic' writer. In an article in *Sociology of Diaspora: A Reader*, Roza Tsagrousianou holds:

> ... diaspora should be seen not as given communities, a logical, albeit deterritorialized, extension of an ethnic or national group, but as imagined communities, continuously reconstructed and reinvented (101).

There is a need to look at diaspora as a community deeply involved in the dynamics of reconstituting the self that finds itself in variance with not only the world around, but also the world within.

The present Arab-American literary scene consists of works of writers like Naomi Shihab Nye, Evelyn Shakir, Laila Halabi, Joseph Geha, Diana Abu-Jaber, Mohja Khaf, to name a few. There is a marked ascendancy of women's voice as they define themselves and demand to be perceived in their own terms. Condemned to occupy the subordinate status in the culture they are born into as well as the culture of adoption, they emerge as doubly besieged group. As writers, like their male counterparts, they too seek to transcend the constraining nomenclature of 'ethnic' writer. As women, they are striving for recognition as much from within the community as without. Finding a voice through creative endeavours and dismantling the prevalent stereotypes of Arab womanhood emerge as concomitants of identity construction arising from hybrid, immigrant sensibility. Amal Abdulrazek, in her article about contemporary Arab-American women writers and the power of story telling, asserts:

> Although ethnicity has often been associated with an exotic otherness or with a sense of authenticity that might be attributed to minority cultures or alien religions, contemporary Arab-American women

> writers emphasize hybridity and diaspora, rather than roots, as a primary means of resisting essentializing identity politics. Their work shifts away from narrow identity politics determined by static notions of race and gender towards a rearticulated politics of difference (2).

Diana Abu-Jaber in her writings articulates the issues that confront the Arab-American immigrants. The concept of identity born of the split vision of hybrid consciousness is problematized in her novels. Daughter of a Jordanian father and American mother, though born in America, she developed affiliations with Jordan during her stay there as a child. Abu-Jaber inherited the legacy of divided loyalties to Jordan, the country that her father wanted her to think of as 'home', and America as the country where she chose to live and work. In an interview with Ramona Koval, referring to the conflict experienced, Diana Abu-Jaber says: 'So I inherited this confusion about identity, appearance and belonging .... I think that's partly why I became a writer, it gives me a forum, it gives me a way to work on and chew over some of these questions and look at them more directly'. Her personal dilemma as a second generation immigrant is explored and interrogated in her novels where she incorporates material from her own life.

Diana perceives identity as multilayered, and characters in her novels emerge as conglomeration of various factors: gender, age, profession, social standing, physical appearance etc., etc. Different strands converge to form a larger, at times, paradoxical, yet comprehensible picture. Identity construction takes place as it runs through and connects with awareness of racism, ethnicity, hybridity, feminism and violence. She highlights the contradictions by focusing on the binaries inherent in the Arab-American immigrant situation: the binaries of preservation of difference and assimilation, of xenophobia and acculturation.

Arabian Jazz, Diana's first novel, published in 2003, delineates the experience of being an Arab-American at times in humorous, and at others, somber tone. The work is a serious attempt to look at the idiosyncrasies and strengths of Arab community as a whole, under the garb of tongue-in-cheek humour. It tells the story of a Jordanian immigrant Matussem, struggling to establish his identity along with raising two daughters Jemorah and Melvina, who like him, are fighting their own battles. Besides interrogating the opposing pulls of the 'old' and the 'new' and the resultant divided loyalty that haunts the immigrant father, racism and marginalization with discrimination based on skin colour results in a sense of alienation, of not belonging and being an outsider. Jemorah, one of the daughters, is victimized by other children in the school bus: 'The other children taunted Jem because of her strange name, her darker skin ... she remembered the sensation of their hands on her body as they teased her, a rippling hatred running over her arms, legs, through her hair' (92). Racism has percolated down to the world of children rendering hopes for future congenial co-existence suspect.

To the empowered white community in America, Negroes and Arabs are almost the same. One is 'nigger' for them, while the other is a 'sand nigger' (99). Homogenization and diminution of Arabs as a community results. They become the butt of racist humour, and sometimes the source of fear and suspicion when demonized as the 'outsider'. Diana also raises the issue of hybridity through the two daughters. Jemorah, the elder daughter, can empathize with the sense of loss experienced by her father: 'In Jem's dreams the moon became Jordan, the place from where her father came from. Her father was a gazelle and he waited by black water's edge staring at the moon' (77). Her own sense of alienation makes her decide to marry a cousin Nassir, till he demystifies her by pointing out—'There is nothing unique or magical about the Middle East; it shares xenophobias and violences with all the rest of the world!' (329) Diana takes up the issue of racist predilection in America in her other works *Crescent* (2004) and *The Language of Baklava* (2006) too.

The othering of Arabs is accompanied by stereotyping. However, the writer judiciously presents the stereotyped notion held by both Arabs as well as Americans of each other. Through her works Diana attempts to rewrite the image of Arabs residing in America. She contests the stereotypes of Arab men and women. Men, though impulsive and at times crafty, are depicted as family-oriented, sensitive and well-mannered. Women are not necessarily domesticated, subjugated and unenlightened. Diana explores interpersonal relationships to explode the stereotypes. *Arabian Jazz* deals with father-daughter relationship while *Crescent* is a story of love and family commitment that also takes into account the experiences of exile, displacement and loneliness. *The Language of Baklava*, as the title indicates, is a food memoir. Cooking becomes a medium of creativity, of cultural expression, reaching out and building bridges. The last novel, *Origin* (2007), though a thriller departs from writer's preoccupation with culture and immigrant experience, it has search for roots, of reconstituting personal history as the chief thrust of the work. All the novels are attempts of the writer at writing the self, be it individual or one that borders on becoming representative through extension and association.

Hybridity is explored through the second-generation Arab-Americans of mixed parentage. Fathers are Arab while mothers are American, in keeping with the background that the writer herself hails from. The autobiographical elements abound as writer depicts the plight of children of such union. The split in their identity gets highlighted with Americans looking at them as coloured, and their own family nagging them for not behaving like proper Arab women. In an interview with Eddie Taylor, Diana refers to the hold Jordan has on her inspite of her decision to live in America, and says: 'Yet in Jordan I don't really feel Jordanian, in America I don't feel American'. The irrepresible Aunt Fatima, in *Arabian Jazz*, rejects the underdog position of an immigrant and aspires for best of both the worlds: 'She lived among Americans, in places they had built, among their people, but despite this she wants to keep herself, her family, and a few friends apart from the rest. She wanted what the Americans had, but at the same time she would never relax her hold on herself. It was not appropriate to mingle. Americans had the money, but Arabs, ah! They had the food, the culture, the etiquette, the ways of being and seeing and understanding how life was meant to be lived' (360).

In most of her novels Diana reconstructs the past from the female perspective. In *Arabian Jazz* it is through the elder daughter Jemorah's memory that her mother's plight of being in an intercultural marriage is reconstructed. The American mother Nora is uncomfortable in family gatherings and feels like an outsider. Metussem, the Jordanian husband is aware of his wife's discomfort: 'There were times when he saw her feeling his family and friends at their parties; she would serve them without speaking, vanishing into the kitchen or bathroom or bedroom, curling into herself like jinni disappearing into air, telling him when he came for her, it was too much, the food and the music and the language rushing into the walls of her head' (189). The trauma arising from cultural differences during transactions in interpersonal relationships is experienced by both, Americans as well as Arabs. Gendered memory is activated to question levels of marginalization of women and the violence perpetrated against them. Fatima, the aunt in *Arabian Jazz,* is haunted by the memory of aiding her mother bury alive unwanted baby girls when she herself was a child. She and her mother are as much the victims of patriarchal society as the helpless infants. *Crescent* too has a female perspective, while *The Language of Baklava* revolves around the memory of an Arab-American girl growing up in a family where father and food play very important role. The American mother is as much an outsider within the family and relatives as Arabs are in America. *Origin* too is about remembering and recovering the past. As the novel unfolds, there is a progressive unraveling of the repressed memory. Thus, by putting the past in context of the present there is an attempt to create a new self, an identity that is based on the evershifting reality of lived experience.

Diana draws heavily from the immigrant experience in America. The situation of conflict arises as much from the geographical, cultural, psychological dislocation as from the racial discrimination experienced. The resultant identity crisis not only leads to search for roots but also initiates rethinking the concept itself. Hybridity, the inevitable yet contested aspect of immigrant experience, gives rise to construction of 'mosaic identity'. Referring to the predicament of the second generation hybrid Arab-American sisters, Jemorah and Melvina in *Arabian Jazz*, their cousin observes:

> ... you are born homeless. Bedouins, not your immigrant parents. You are torn in two. You get two looks at a world. You may be never perfect fit, but you see far more than most ever do (330).

Finally it is the richness of experience that redeems the diasporic consciousness as it inscribes the beleaguered self into existence through creative endeavour.

REFERENCES

Abdelrazek, Amal. 'Scherazad's Legacy: Arab-American Women Writers and the Resisting, Healing, and Connecting Power of their Storytelling." *The MIT Electronic Journal of Middle East Studies*. Vol.5, Spring 2005.

Abinader, Elimaz. "Children of AL Mahjar: Arab American Literature Spans a Century." http://usinfo.state.gov/journals/itsv/0200/ijse/abinader.html.

Abu-Jaber, Diana. *Arabian Jazz*. New York: W.W. Norton and Company, 2003.

—. *Crescent*. New York: W.W. Norton and Company, 2004.

—. *Origin*. New York: W.W. Norton and Company, 2007.

—. *The Language of Baklava*. New York; Anchor Books, 2006.

Gibran, Kahlil. "Sand and Foam". In *The Greatest Works of Kahlil Gibran*. Mumbai: Jaico Publishing House, 2003.

Graham, Maryemma. ed. *The Cambridge Companion to The African American Novel*. UK: Cambridge University Press, 2004.

Koval, Ramola. Interview with Diana Abu-Jaber. http://www.abc.net.au/in/arts/bwriting/stories/51409284.htm.

Parmeswaran, Uma. "Dispelling the Spells of Memory". *Writing the Diaspora: Essays on Culture and Identity*. Jaipur: Rawat Publications, 2007.

Taylor, Eddie. 'Best of Both Worlds'. Interview with Diana Abu-Jaber. http://www.sway-magazine.com/daj.html.

Tsagarousianou, Roza. "Reevaluating 'Diaspora': Connectivity, Communication and Imagination in a Globalised World". *Sociology of Diaspora: A Reader* Vol. 1. Eds. Ajay Kumar Sahoo and Brij Maharaj. Jaipur: Rawat Publications, 2007.

CHAPTER 17

Writing as Healing

Unless by Carol Shields

Uma Mahadevan

Unless (2002) is a novel about the healing effect of life stories. For Reta Winters, the narrator, writing the story of her own grief becomes 'a very small poultice to hold up against (her) damaged self, but better, I have been persuaded, than no comfort at all' (2). Reta has a busy and active life as a mother, wife and writer. Apart from working on a translation of the memoirs of a feminist poet, she is also writing her own second novel. But rather than telling us about her busy, happy life filled with sunshine, it is while telling us about an *interruption* in this life—what Reta calls her 'period of great unhappiness and loss' caused by a family crisis—that she makes some valuable discoveries. These discoveries, about herself and her writing, offer her a way to affirm and heal herself. 'We are real only in our moments of recognition' (84). Reta reminds herself, quoting words that she has read.

As a novel about writing, *Unless* introspects self-consciously on the choices made in the creative process, and the implications of those choices. Although well-known as a translator of a Holocaust survivor and feminist poet Danielle Westerman's work, Reta acknowledges that her own fiction is generally regarded as light and even frivolous. But when her new editor tries to bring into her work the too-clever techniques of contemporary publishing—including the effort to shift the moral centre of the novel from the female protagonist to the male—Reta struggles to maintain the integrity of her vision.

Unless is about an unexpected turn in the plot of Reta's own life story. Reta lives with her doctor husband Tom outside Toronto. Being children of the sixties, they never had a formal marriage, but Reta did legally adopt Tom's last name. With a comfortable house, three daughters and a friendly dog, it looks as though they have the ideal happy family life—until the title of the novel, *Unless*, brings the turn in the plot. One day Reta hears that her first daughter Norah has dropped out of college as well as abandoned her relationship to sit on a Toronto street corner behind a signboard that reads: 'Goodness'.

The word is not printed on a page in a book as part of the vast publishing industry (of which Reta is a part), but scripted by hand in black ink—itself an act of protest and resistance, a claim to restore meaning to a word that has lost its value in an age of irony. On seeing this word Reta (who is aware of her position as a published writer: 'words are my business', she remarks), is at a loss. As novelist and translator, she has always imagined that she has control over her world. But now she wonders what could have brought about this unexpected turn of events: 'How did this part of the narrative happen? We know it didn't rise out of the ordinary plot lines of a life story. An intelligent and beautiful girl from a loving family grows up in Orangetown, Ontario, her mother's a writer, her father's a doctor, and then she goes off the track' (9).

Unless has a layered technique interspersing several strands of narrative. The novel is made up of some dozen short chapters with titles that are not even phrases but fragments of phrases, staccato bursts of language: 'Here's' (the first chapter), 'Nearly', 'Once', 'Whatever', and so on. Towards the end of the novel, Reta explains the reason for these odd chapter titles as part of her effort to discover meaning:

> A life is full of isolated events, but these events, if they are to form a coherent narrative, require odd pieces of language to cement them together, little chips of grammar (mostly adverbs or prepositions) that are hard to define, since they are abstractions of location or relative position, words like *therefore, else, other, also, thereof, theretofore, instead, otherwise, despite, already,* and *not yet (208).*

There are three categories of chapters: first, those which form Reta's direct narrative, where she recounts the events of her life; second, letters composed by her to important men (but never posted); and third, chapters that tell us about the progression of Reta's work-in-progress and the destinies of the characters in that novel. Although the chapters often look like brief reflections based, sometimes, on little more than a scrap of memory or a line of dialogue, they also give the impression of being part of the larger architectural design of the novel. Writing is the art of making wise choices to find this design and draw meaning from experience. The epigraph from George Eliot emphasizes this need for selection, without which the sheer vastness of experience would become incomprehensible: 'If we had a keen vision and feeling of all ordinary human life, it would be like hearing the grass grow and the squirrel's heartbeat and we should die of that roar that lies on the other side of that silence.'

The novel begins in *medias res*, or rather, opens not with Reta's happy, sunny life so far, but with the loss that will define the 'new life' to which her grief has brought her. The opening chapter, titled 'Here's', is her attempt to 'count (her) blessings' (with painful bluntness, she calls it a 'repellent strategy' but makes the effort nevertheless), in which she enumerates the stages in her evolution as a writer so far (1). It is an exposition of Reta's writing milestones, from her first translation of a book of poetry by a French-Canadian feminist poet to the novel that she is still in the midst of planning. Through the narrative, she will continue to describe to us what is happening in the 'lives' of her characters in this work-in-progress, describing to us the stages of the writing process and the choices it requires. By the end of the novel, Reta's experience of sadness affects her resolve about the destinies of her characters, and leads her to a sad ending for the third novel that she plans to write.

Although she has been reasonably prolific, writing is, for Reta, an activity hastily undertaken in the midst of motherhood. 'My macramé,' says Reta wryly (3), acknowledging the place that writing gets in her life, in the midst of bringing up children and running a busy house. Even while telling us about the converted boxroom that becomes her workspace, and about the luxury of being paid for her work—the holiday in France, the summer spent reading novels—she is diffident, even self-deprecatory about her work, even though Westerman assures her that translation is 'an act of originality' (4). Writing about the Russian icons, Reta adds that it is impossible to be 'pseudo' about 'innocent paintings'. When she is busy with work, she talks about having 'lost a year' (5). And then, almost shyly, she reveals her own aspiration as a creative writer in control of a fictional world of her own: 'I want to write a novel … . About something happening. About characters moving against a "there" ' (8). It is at this point—looking back indulgently at her sense of being in control of her world—that Reta encounters the reality of her loss again. 'Such innocence,' (8) she tells herself about her worldview at that time.

For Reta, writing is, like motherhood, a profoundly creative vocation, filled with wonder and miraculousness, a love for words and characters, a sense of their need to be nurtured, an awareness of their possibilities, and an intimate concern with their destinies. Although writing is an activity performed in isolation, it is an effort to reach out to others. Reta's writing group provides a friendly, supportive environment that sustains the members through the isolation of the writing process. Writing links Reta to other writers, *genres*, and influences; to the heft of history and the literary tradition itself. Reta refers to her first short story, 'Icon', written as a response to an exhibition of Russian art, as 'rather Jamesian' (3), while her writer friend Gwen recalls Keats's sonnet on Chapman's Homer.

The first volume of their women writers' collective, tellingly titled 'Incursions and Interruptions', is an exercise in self-publishing. Optimistically they titled their publishing effort the 'Stepping Stone Press', hoping to move on to what Reta refers to as 'authentic publishing' in course of time. But now, as a published and moderately successful writer, Reta is aware of writing as an industry with its own powerful compulsions—involving a series of processes from editing and publishing, to the marketing promotions, interviews, signing tours, reviews, and academic discussions. She knows the routine:

> Suck in your breath, let your face go numb, evaluate the feelings of those who depend on you (agent, publisher, editor, that nice Sheila person who does publicity, and of course Danielle Westerman), and perform again and again like the tuned-up athlete you are, the fit physical specimen that each new book demands, then move on to the next task. (20)

But Reta is also aware of the worthwhile aspects of the business of writing and reading as ways of reaching out to the larger community. She finds a moment of bonding with the group of fellow citizens in the library reading room which is like 'a private club, with everyone so relaxed and polite and obeying the rules ... sharing public space, at one with each other in our need for retreat and for the printed word ...' (29). For Reta, immersing herself in the writing of others is like entering a storehouse of experience and wisdom. Faced with Norah's baffling one-word message, Reta instinctively turns to the library for answers, checking out a book called 'The Goodness Gap'. She also knows the special worth of fiction in helping to make sense of the world (reading novels, she remarks, would make the insensitive Willow Halliday a less boring person). The librarians keep a set of books for Reta, novels 'that describe the unwrittenness of unremarkable men and women. Their instinct is to keep these books flowing towards those who have lost touch with the "real world" ' (26).

At one level, then, there is the extraneous business of helping books to find their readership; but at a more fundamental level, writing is an organic process for Reta, an act of courage that requires as much honesty, sincerity and integrity as anything else in the world, if not more. For Reta, the novel originates with 'a seed' (9): two characters, a setting, temperaments, jobs, and a title. Before her experience of life going out of control, her fiction has a definite design ('Naturally the novel would have a happy ending' 10). But in her new experience of loss, the novel not only catches her unawares ('How did this part of the narrative happen?' (8), but becomes something more dangerous: it is 'the poison of the printed page' (11). And it is almost a prophecy: 'I'm desperate to know how the story will turn out' (11).

With her own life going out of control, Reta still seeks some measure of control in her fictional world. But after her experience of loss, Reta is reconciled to let her fiction become a more measured orchestral work, even an oil painting ('Seated Woman. Woman At Rest'); 'a book that's willing to live in one room if necessary'. Finally, she sees her novel as destiny: 'It will be a sadder book than the others, and shorter' (213). She is aware of the novelistic device of coincidence, of how even in a novel nothing happens in a contrived fashion—but she also knows that it has to happen organically, out of the internal logic of who the characters are, and what kind of lives they lead; and that such destinies are inescapable.

Above all, writing is a form of healing: 'a small poultice' as Reta calls it, but better than nothing. Although Tom is also in the healing profession, there are some forms of suffering that respond more to Reta's form of therapy rather than the ways of conventional medicine. For Reta, writing through her pain is a means of better comprehending her loss and through this process, better constructing and healing herself. Her pain is represented in terms of something lost, while happiness was, for her, 'the lucky pane of glass you carry in your head. It takes all your cunning just to hang on to it, and once it's smashed you have to move into a different sort of life' (1).

The process of repair and self-renovation begins by exposing old and buried wounds and reflecting upon how they were caused. Confronting her loss directly, Reta instinctively uses language to repair and reconstruct herself. In the ladies' washroom in a Toronto restaurant, her head is 'a ringing vessel of pain' (44), but her words are ready. The moment she adds her voice to the graffiti on the cubicle door— 'My heart is broken,' she writes, adding the picture of a heart broken in two—she feels a physical sense of relief, the 'release of pressure around my ribs ... for the first time in weeks I was able to take a deep breath' (45).

Other women also choose to respond to grief by retreating into themselves. Norah withdraws into silence, as does Reta's mother-in-law, Lois (and even Danielle Westerman chooses to remain silent about her mother's role in her life). Silence involves withdrawal from the world; but writing helps Reta to avoid such a withdrawal by requiring her to focus, engage with, and pay attention to the world around her. She seeks to understand Norah's act in the language with which she is most familiar, the 'textual archaeology' of the street corner which has its own place in Toronto's heritage of protest (8). She searches for meanings in her own dreams. She tries to read Norah's face for feelings or recognition as much as she tries to read the cause of the scars on her daughter's arms. She tries to interpret Norah's response to a Flaubert course in college, where Norah ached for the way in which Madame Bovary was 'forced to surrender her place as the moral centre of the novel' (144).

At the same time, Reta begins to look deeply at the rich sprawl of daily life, the concrete detail—the 'long August evenings, the splash of amber light ... the medallion leaves that flutter their round ghost shadows' (12). She pays attention to objects in her house—the oak banister, the crisp napkins—not only for their functional usefulness in her life but as well for their warm loveliness in themselves, and the sense of order that they represent. She is not only searching for some hidden meaning that might explain Norah's sudden act, but also, eventually, finding a renewed gratitude and appreciation for the beauty and rich textures of the world.

Life stories are not only about telling but equally about listening and asking questions. Questions are crucial 'You are allowed to forget ... unless we ask questions', (210), and the most important question is, at the same time, the simplest one.

Arthur Springer gets Reta's mother-in-law to talk about herself by asking her simply and directly: 'Tell me all about yourself, Lois' (196).

Opening up a life story to discussion and scrutiny can lead to new discoveries. Reta feels that the prose of Danielle Westerman's memoir, although 'larger, more rapturous, more self-forgetful than anything she's ever written before' (10), is lacking in something, because Westerman writes as one who is alone in the world. Reta asks Westerman about this unexplained gap in the narrative: 'point-blank ... what it was that had interrupted her childhood' (210). It is this question that leads Westerman finally to acknowledge her mother and begin writing about her, bringing together her identities as daughter and writer.

Although Reta looks at the larger questions—relativity, world events, the close finish in the 2000 US Presidential elections—her loss has turned her attention to what really matters. 'Tom and I have views about the news, which we continue to express, even though we know how inconsequential the unfolding of political events is. People enter and exit the world; that's the real news' (130).

As we empathize with the sorrow of others, writing provides a way of healing for others too. When the marriage of Colin and Marietta broke up, Marietta left her diaries—her life stories—for him to read. 'He had had no idea ... that she had been unhappy all these years' (14). Colin tries to reconstruct his life story by never discussing Marietta with their friends, in an attempt to 'erase' her from his life. It is painful for him to read the revelations in her diaries, but his pain is the necessary beginning of the healing of their relationship. When they finally reconciled, it is on the basis of a shared understanding.

And as Reta tells the story of her grief, she learns to introspect and draw courage from her reflection. There is a sense of optimism at the end of the novel. Norah is back at home, and things have started looking better. Reta's second novel, the work that she began writing in the first chapter, has also reached a 'whimsical conclusion ... everything is neatly wrapped up at the end' (211). By bringing order and meaning to the strands of narrative, writing affirms a sense of meaning in life. But Reta also knows, as a novelist, that happy endings are fragile things: 'I have bundled up each of the loose narrative strands, but what does such fastidiousness mean? It doesn't mean that all will be well for ever and ever, amen; it means that for five minutes a balance has been achieved at the margin of the novel's thin textual plane ...' (211).

REFERENCE

Shields, Card. *Unless*, London and New York: Fourth Estate. 2002.

CHAPTER 18

The Vagaries of Memory and the Shaping of the Self

Carol Shields' *The Stone Diaries*

Mini Nanda

> *Our lives would be intolerable without some predicate, some ballast of identity, to provide a context for the wings of thought and action that constitute our instantaneous selves. We may be small in space ... we are each of us giants in the dimension of time.*
>
> —Daniel Albright

Carol Shields moved to Canada at the age of twenty-two; after studying in England at the University of Exeter, she did her post graduation from the University of Ottawa. She started publishing poetry in her thirties and wrote her first novel, *Small Ceremonies* in 1976, at the age of 41. Over the next three decades she authored some twenty books, including plays, poetry, essays, short fiction, novels, a book of criticism on Susanna Moodie (1976), and as she always loved biographies, a biography on Jane Austen in 2001, for which she won the Charles Taylor prize for literary non-fiction.

Carol Shields worked as an academic and taught at the Universities of British Columbia, Ottawa and at Manitoba. She became the Chancellor of the University of Winnipeg in 1996 where she lived for fifteen years and used it as a backdrop to her fiction, most remarkably in *Republic of Love* (1992) which was made into a film directed by Deepa Mehta, in 2003. Her novel *Swann* was made into a film in 1996, *Larry's Party* 1997 was adapted for a musical stage play. Her works has been translated into twenty-two languages.

In her two Anthologies both entitled *Dropped Threads* (2001) the women contributors both well-known and the unknown were encouraged to write those experiences they were normally unable to express. Her experience had made her realize that women were naturally involved in protecting themselves and the people around them that they felt the compulsion, to remain silent on certain issues. Shields made the unique effort to record the lives of women, whose lives were thought to be of no value, except housekeeping and playing bridge.

This deep reverence for the untold stories of middle-class, ordinary women led to the fictive autobiographical novel entitled *The Stone Diaries* 1993, for which she won the Pulitzer Prize in 1995, and Canada's Governor General Award for fiction. The genesis of the novel was in Carol Shields' interest in the notion of autobiography, the idea of women's life stories where she felt that a lot is erased from their lives due to their own hesitation and attitude or because of societal pressure.

Atwood in *Curious Pursuits* writes that fiction is a site where individual memory and experience, and collective memory and experience come together (209); she further expresses the view that history and novel cannot be written without memory (213). In this way in *The Stone Diaries* the narrator's memory is linked with other characters and events.

It is often believed that autobiography is a very personal form of self expression, yet as Sudhir Kakar writes that there is a school of thought that holds that nobody writes without an audience in mind, though the definition of such an audience may vary. While pointing out that the dichotomy between private and public audiences is false, Kakar stresses that an individual writes for the other, which may be one's split or divided self, the mother-in-law one hates, or for a specific public audience. Whether the audience actually reads the text is not of any consequence, what is relevant is that an individual writes for, against or to another. An outside agent provides the impetus for the act of writing and the sense of audience whether defined or indeterminate is always present (Karlekar, 1991: 17–18).

The Stone Diaries is the fictional life story of an ordinary woman, Daisy Goodwill Flett—who makes an extraordinary attempt to tell her story from her calamitous birth to death. It is not a diary in the conventional sense, as no regular entries are made. The ten chapters deal with ten or more years of the different phases of her life as given by the author: 'Birth' 1905, 'Childhood' 1946, 'Marriage' 1927 and interestingly after 'Marriage' the next chapter is titled 'Love' 1936, 'Motherhood' and so on till her death where the year is not actually documented, it is 'somewhere' in the 1990s. There is a family tree also and documentation and photographs which do not always correspond with her characters. Shields has unabashedly admitted to using her own children's photographs for Daisy's grandchildren.

How does an ordinary life assume significance? What shapes and defines it? Does it belong to her or to the scores of people who also shape it? What is fact and what is fiction in the narration? Can we separate one from the other? These questions assume significance as the text unfolds. There are multiple narrative voices in *The Stone Diaries* and the fictional life is interspersed with documentation; various characters share their memories and interpret a single life, in the process other stories unfold as well. Each voice belongs to different individuals, together these lives gain meaning.

The epigraph taken from 'The Grandmother Cycle', by Judith Downing in *The Stone Diaries* reveals the richness of the unfolding: nothing she did or said was quite what she mean but still her life could be called a monument shaped in a slant of available light and set to the movement of possible music.

In 'Self-Narratives: True and False', Ulric Neisser (1994) notes that it is remarkable that people remember what happened to them, and reconstruct the past events which impinge the present. 'Life narratives are significant because they are one way of defining the self' (1) He feels that self-narratives are a way of defining the self and may not always be true (2). For what one remembers may not be accurate, and people begin their narratives from their birth. Daisy gives us an account of her birth, not just the moment of her arrival into the world, but also the last gasps of her dying mother as well.

Daisy begins her narration from her birth, she 'witnesses it in the kitchen' in 1905, as her mother, Mercy Stone, prepares supper on a boiling hot day. Mercy Stone is an artist at work—a heavy woman of thirty—whose idea of paradise is the kitchen and the food she cooks with great 'artistry'. Daisy tells us that her mother was an orphan at 'Stonewall Orphans' Home', where each foundling was given the surname 'Stone'. Her mother's fine hair and hazel eyes suggest an Ukrainian or Icelandic origin. She became elephantine by age twenty. It was a rhyme in the orphanage that 'Mercy Stone weighs forty stone' (30). Daisy writes that her mother, Mercy Stone Goodwill, gave the child the last of her breath, 'Its the wing beat of breath I reach out for. Even now I claim it absolutely … the fact of her final breath … freezing against my sealed eyelids and saying open, open' (40).

In her utter helplessness, Daisy mocks at history, that paltry slice of time, she feels, deserves the name 'accident' not history, which had brought so many people together, at the time of her birth. In retrospect, to that amazing moment, Daisy comments with wisdom:

'Life is an endless recruiting of witnesses. It seems we need to be observed in our postures of extravagance or shame, we need attention paid to us. Our own memory is altogether too cherishing, which is the kindest thing I can say for it, other accounts are required, other perspectives' (37).

Daniel Albright in 'Literary and Psychological Models of the Self' (1994), notes that each one of us carries 'a videotape of our identity' (21). Albright calls it a 'time doll', with one's own features, which keeps taking shape from one's infancy, becoming more marked with each significant experience and it culminates in our present. 'We feel an amazing intimacy with this "time doll"—not only do we cherish it as the dearest thing in our lives, but it cherishes us as well, it supports us, it defends us against the thinness, boredom and futility of the immediate present ...' (21). This 'time doll' is our individual self which defines our identity from time to time as it changes and takes different shapes.

Neisser's view becomes pertinent that autobiographical memory is best taken with a grain of salt. The self that is remembered in the present is not the historical self of yesterday, but only a reconstructed version (8). Daisy too recreates the past from the moment of her birth. It is a creative reconstruction of the 'Time doll', of the self, through the varied phases of one's life.

Daisy candidly admits at the outset that the recounting of a life is a lie, 'I admit the truth of this; even our own stories are obscenely distorted; it is a wonder really that we keep faith with the simple container of our existence' (28). Nevertheless we all cherish our stories because they define us, give us an identity and fulfill us in many ways. The art of writing, of narrating the self could well be compared to the structuring of the tower by Daisy's father—Cuyler Goodwill—his monument of love for his dead wife—Mercy. The tower becomes a tourist spot in the village of Tyndall, Manitoba, where it is sometimes called the *Taj Mahal*, a monument to love. Patterns incised on this minaret seem to evade the eye; one would have to stand at a certain distance and in a particular light to make them out. The impediment is part of the charm for him, 'what he carves will remain half-hidden, half-exposed, and as such will reflect the capriciousness of the revealed world' (64).

Daniel Albright (1994) further cautions us that the remembered self is a fragile construction (21). He adds that the 'time doll' is after all just a doll, it cannot and must not relieve us of the responsibility of self-analysis and self-reflection. In Daisy's detailed account, there is no self-analysis on her own part, no reflective assessment of her life. Nevertheless the narrative is interesting, at times her close friends do analyse her personal action, when they tell their account. As Albright points out, the problem in narrating the remembered self comes from three directions. First, the brokenness of memory, it is not a continuous flow, secondly, the problem of affirming that all memories pertain to the same self, and the third problem arises from the near impossibility of ascertaining that the subject is an object (22). But one can add that this does not necessarily limit or fictionalise the self. Memory is personal, biased, broken, but it does shape the contours of one's life. The remembered self is like Kafka's Great Wall of China, in Albright's view it is not continuous, but is in short stretches, with more holes than bricks (22–23).

The story that Daisy tells, along with the stories of her neighbours, aunt, friends and the intervention of the author herself will be something mysterious and half revealed, with all the holes in her memory. Were her childhood years lonely? Did her foster mother, Clarentine Flett, who was her parents' neighbour, fill the vacuum of a mother? What about her school in Winnipeg? The novel does not plumb the depths of her inner life, even though it chronicles the life in great detail. Daisy's foster mother, Clarentine, dies when she was eleven years old, she is re-united with her father, Cuyler Goodwill, and moves from Winnipeg to the US—Bloomington—Indiana. On the train for three full days, the silent, lonely man (her father), becomes an orator in the presence of his daughter. Cuyler tells her his own life story.

Daisy's father had built a tower in memory of his dead wife Mercy, but when Daisy's first husband dies in a state of deep inebriation on their honeymoon, Daisy never tells the story to another soul. She is completely reticent about it and not altogether an unhappy young widow. Her second marriage with Barker Flett, her foster uncle, is both an escape from her father's house and from a life that had reached a dead end. Her husband is twenty-three years her senior, he is closer to her father in age. Matrimony is a swirl of housekeeping, rearing, cooking and gardening. Much like her mother, Mercy, Daisy also is accommodating and sedate about her life. 'The debris of her married life rains down around her, the anniversaries, pregnancies, vacations, meals ... crowding out the dramatic, some would say incestuous—origin of her relationship with her partner in marriage' (191).

In contrast to her chaotic life her garden is lush, grand and intimate, English in its charm, French in its orderliness, Japanese in its economy, and in a mocking way, the writer notes that there is something too, in the sinuous path which is full of grave intelligence and a kind of wit (195). One wonders if her garden can be substituted for writing of her self as well. There is sunlight and beauty in her account, when she describes her mother, Mercy. Partly this picture has been built from imagination and hearsay. The rippling generosity of her flesh, the clear floury look of her bare arms, her bread slices which were a miracle of sweetness and crispness, richly satisfying. Then the sinuous curving of the trajectory, the presence of the timid besotted young man (her father) and the heavy immense woman (her mother). Remembering them Daisy is overcome even in her crowded marriage with gusts of grief and loneliness. Many may yearn to know the true state of her garden, but she wants to be part of its mysteries, she perhaps understands only a quarter of its green secrets, it demands nothing of her, her name or history, it is her dearest child (196).

The narrative technique is varied and takes up different styles, there is narration, letters, other people's point-of-view and photographs as well. The first segment 'Birth' in the novel is in the first person; the rest of the narration is taken up by the omniscient voice of the author herself, with inputs by way of letters. Letters are written by Daisy's husband, friends, relatives to her under the title 'Work 1955–1964', which run into about thirty pages.

'Theory' or versions by her friends and family members; are again in the first person. The versions are not very disparate, and they contribute to make a whole picture, which is multilayered. In the middle of the novel the author warns the readers that

Daisy is nct very reliable when it comes to details of her life (148), much of what she says could be speculative and exaggerated, the writer wonders if her first mother-in-law, Mrs Arthur Hoad, was really as cruel and heartless as described by Daisy and the reader in turn asks why couldn't she be so? The writer gives her assessment of Daisy:

> Daisy Goodwill's perspective is off ... she imposes the voice of the future on the events of the past, causing all manner of wavy distortion. She takes great jumps in time .... She does insist on showing herself in a sunny light, hardly ever giving us a glimpse of those dark premonitions we all experience. And, oh dear, she is cursed with the lonely woman's romantic imagination and thus can support only happy endings. (148)

When Daisy left as a young girl with her father, Barker Flett her foster uncle, wrote six letters a year for twenty-two years to her, making it an impressive total of one hundred and thirty-two letters, fighting against his own lacerating loneliness. The author writes that in her letters to Barker she adopted a frivolous girlish tone and preserved all his letters. After her marriage to Barker, the writer tells us that Daisy gave up the practice of keeping a private journal, she lost her diary. One of the reasons for this could be the author decides to take the journal out of the hands of unreliable narrator and take complete control in telling the story.

In a poetic way Carol Shields writes about the inner life of Daisy, her panic at some loss of memory:

> And yet within her anxiety, secured there like a gemstone, she carries the cool and curious power of occasionally seeing the world vividly .... The narrative maze opens and permits her to pass through. She may be crowded out of her life... but she possesses, as a compensatory gift, the startling ability to draft alternate versions. (190)

Daisy combats her tears and loneliness, the pressure of the unruly secret of her childhood, and the special moment of closeness to her mother, and the sense of reversal as if she has given birth to her mother. Perhaps the recounting of her birth and her mother's short span of thirty years, combined with Daisy's own nurturing spirit, gives her the feeling of mothering her own dead mother. A dramatic reversal is brought about as Daisy imaginatively reconstructs her mother bringing her back to life. This re-birth fills up the vacuum in Daisy's life. Her three children while they play revive their own memories, 'take turns comparing and repeating their separate and shared memories and shivering with pleasure every time a fresh fragment from the past is unearthed' (174).

In the chapter entitled 'Sorrow' Daisy sinks into depression, after her second husband's death and loss of her vocation – her garden columns – are suddenly discontinued, several characters give their versions in the first person narration once again of their views about her depression.

Charles Rycroft (1972) observes that the psychoanalytical literature is unanimous in regarding melancholic depression as a psychological form of mourning. As an emotion it expresses gloominess and loss of spirit. All the symptoms are seen in Daisy's condition. Her eldest child Alice admits in her version that she (Alice) had been a mean, cruel and a self-centred child (234). Then Alice makes up her mind to learn to be kind, she says first she burnt up her old diaries and her letters which she felt were full of gush and artifice.

When Daisy sees Alice destroying her personal records, she warns Alice that she would regret it later. The act of destroying diaries kept till a certain point of time is a way of letting the past go, to make an attempt to reinvent the self, similar to what Alice's mother did after the death of the first husband. Alice saw her mother as a composed person who kept a neat and ordered house, as she was twenty-three years younger than her father; her mother, Daisy, was a permanent tenant in the tower of girlhood (236). After her father's death, her work in the horticulture magazine gave her mother a sense of purpose, 'But then, presto, she became Mrs Green Thumb. Her old self-slipped off like an oversized jacket' (239). Daisy's personality changes after her second husband's death, she is fully absorbed in writing horticulture column at the *Recorder* (237). And Alice feels the dismissal from work led to her mother's grief.

Fraidy Hoyt of Bloomington, Indiana, gives her side of the story of Daisy's depression as she was Daisy's school and college friend. Fraidy finds her husband an 'epicene presence' in Daisy's life. Fraidy breezily states that once in a while a family has to surrender itself to an outsider's account. 'A family can get burned in its own fairy dust, and this leads straight ... to the unpacking of lies and fiction from its piddly shared scraps of inbred history' (244). She felt that with the Fletts the work ethic was writ large. Daisy may have had a brief flutter after her husband's death with the paper editor, Jay Dudley, and that made her only one and a half bean sprout by Fraidy's account. For Fraidy kept a diary from 1927–1965 of all her fifty-four lovers, she sees herself on the other side of the fence and silently raises a toast to her army of fifty-four lovers. It is Daisy's sexual unfulfilment that Fraidy blames for Daisy's depression. For her the self is shaped and curved like space and that it is through that erotic pleasure one can enter the realm of the ecstatic. Ironically Fraidy drops her little pocket diary with all the cryptic entries in Daisy's house. And Daisy with grave attention mails it back to her.

Cousin Beverly, the unwed mother, and her daughter, Victoria, were given shelter by aunt Daisy. Life presents Daisy with a chance to play foster mother to the teenage niece, and both the niece and her daughter become a part of the family, with their own special place in the house. Beverly is full of admiration and love for her aunt and she feels that Daisy's three children, with their unruly behaviour and selfishness, had taken a toll on their mother's health.

Daisy's son, Warren, a budding musician is bewildered by the erudite essay she wrote in college. He wonders where his mother's intellectual ease and energy vanished. As a son he feels cheated out of her other self; he wonders how much more cheated she would be feeling. Warren judges that it is the squandering of herself, her talents that his mother is mourning (252).

The most astonishing account in the chapter is that of the 'Old Jew' Abram Gozhde Skutari in Tyndall. His grandson—Skoot Skutari—writes about the early life of his grandfather, a self-made man, a millionaire, founder and owner of a nationwide chain of retail outlets. As a peddler he would peddle his wares in Tyndall, Manitoba, where in spite of the usefulness of his supplies he was despised and called 'Old Jew'. People would scour and scald the room, bedding and the tea cups he had used, no one had the courtesy to ask him his name. He brought help on the summer mid-afternoon in 1905, when Mercy Stone (Daisy's mother) lay sprawled on the kitchen floor. He brought Clarentine Flett, the next door neighbour, and rushed to the only doctor in the village. It was Skutari who sensed the grief in the last glance of the dying mother, he felt the immense loneliness of the child on the kitchen table. He grieved for the newborn and from his pocket he took out an old coin and held it to the head of the baby and blessed her, while he wept all the time. It was a moment of opposites, the signing of the death certificate and the birth certificate, when the whole group stood as one. All the prejudice against the old Jew was washed away by the tears that mingled, and admiration at the fact that Skutari actually had a name and that he could write. After this incident Abram Gozhde (Skutari) felt a surge of renewed energy to face the Royal Bank and acquire the loan, that later set him on the road of amazing success.

Margaret Atwood notes that Shields was conscious of the vagaries of success, and the element of chance in any fortune, she knew about darkness and she held on to light. As she battled with and succumbed to the terminal disease on July 16, 2005 at sixty-eight, Margaret Atwood pays her homage to Carol Shields in these lines:

> And live she did and live she does for as John Keats remarked, every writer has two souls, an earthly one and one that lives on in the world of writing as a voice in the writing itself. It's this voice, astute, compassionate, observant and deeply human, that will continue to speak to her reader everywhere (344).

Alice Munro, her friend and fellow writer, wrote that 'she was just a luminous person, and that would be important and persist even if she hadn't written anything' (341). Atwood feels that human life is a mass of statistics only for statisticians, the rest of the people live in a world of individuals, and most of them are not prominent. Their joys are fully joyful, and their grief real. It was the extraordinariness of ordinary people that was Shields' *forte* (341–342).

In a unique narrative twist the last intervention titled 'Mrs Flett's theory', on Daisy's depression is written by the author on behalf of Daisy. While free advice flew quick and fast around her, the writer reveals that within Daisy there lay, like a sleeping burrowing creature, a certainty that she would recover. 'In a sense I see her as one of life's fortunate, a woman born with a voice that lacks a tragic register. Someone who learned to dig a hole in her own life story' (263). The author writes with conviction that very soon she will slough off her sadness with a hoot of laughter and all her suffering will be washed away.

Carl Jung observes that the greatest and most important problems of life are all fundamentally insoluble ... they can never be solved, but only outgrown. This outgrowing is the raising of one's level of consciousness to some higher or wider interest, and the insoluble problem loses it urgency, it fades out before a new and stronger life tendency. It is not repressed or made unconscious ... but viewed from a higher level of personality, the person is not in it, in a state of conflict and panic but above it (88–89). The problem loses its grip and is surmounted by directing oneself to other commitments. The human self is complex, it does not flow in a continuous stream, beneath the calm surface is the dark depth, which is difficult to plumb, more so to express.

Daisy narrates her life and the unspoken, unvocalized segments take their toll and she sinks into depression. But she emerges out of it, first, by embracing, and then, by distancing herself from her past life, her home and her garden. All the beautiful people and material things she had accumulated are discarded. Towards the end of her life there is an incoherence of speech and thought, the reality of the self is plural, it is still and it is constantly moving, it is one appearance and multiple shifting within. The moment of death is recorded, 'The brilliant room collapses, leaning on a solid block of darkness' (358). Daisy's spirit hovers over the dead body and the narrative records Daisy's response to her death, as it had recorded the moment of her birth. Bemused she watches the body turn to stone. The folds of her dress acquire a stiff calcium decorative border, her eyes stare 'icy as marbles' and in a moment of epiphany she sees, and she seems to understand the 'distress of men and women, and how little they are allowed, finally, to say' (359). It is the moment of the word (Stone) becoming the image (Statue), her last posture as she seems to be transfixed in/as stone is 'Grecian. Quiet. Timeless. Classic' (359). Life is captured and held timeless in Art.

The turning of the human body into stone and Grecian statue, is both ironic and aesthetic. It points to the silencing of a life, which Daisy endeavoured to fashion in her writing and account. It led her to some understanding of the human predicament, of how little could actually be narrated. The rest is silence. The self is not static in life, it grows and memory encodes those moments of growth, some moments are also forgotten or elided by memory. The novelist begins with 'hints and images', not with 'theories and grand schemes' (223). Then the character emerges and Daisy the protagonist and Shields the writer pass the narrative to and fro in a unique technique of telling, raised to the level of aesthetic sculpturing.

REFERENCES

Albright, Danniel. "Literary and Psychological Models of the Self", *The Remembering Self: Construction and Accuracy in the Self-Narratives*. Eds. Ulric Neisser and Robin Fivush. Cambridge: Cambridge University Press, 1994.

Atwood, Margaret. *Curious Pursuits: Occasional Writings*. 1970–2005. Great Britain: Virago, 2005.

Jung, Carl and Richard Wilhelm. *The Secret of the Golden Flower*. Trans. Cary F. Baynes. London and New York, 1931.

Karlekar, Malvika. *Voices From Within: Early Personal Narratives of Bengali Women*. Delhi: OUP, 1991.

Neisser, Ulric, "Self-Narratives: True and False", *Remembering Self: Construction and Accuracy in the Self-Narratives*. Eds. Ulric Neisser ,and Robin Fivush. Cambridge: Cambridge University Press, 1994.

Rycroft, Charles. *A Critical Dictionary of Psychoanalysis*. Penguin, 1972.

Shields, Carol. *Susanna Moodie: Voice and Vision*. Canada: Borealis Press, 1976.

—. *The Stone Diaries*. Toronto: Vintage Books, 1993.

— and Marjorie Anderson. *Dropped Threads: What we Aren't Told*. Vol 1&2. Random House, 2001.

CHAPTER 19

Self within the Shadows of History

Santosh Gupta

Amitav Ghosh locates his characters at the crossroads of historical and political turmoil. Characters of his novels experience the sufferings, struggles and reactions caused by the (post)colonial dislocations and destabilizations. Whether living in India, Burma, Middle East or any European country subjugated people across the world have been compelled to undergo humiliations and sufferings that have had deep impact on their sense of selfhood, dignity and self respect. In depicting these experiences Ghosh's novels foreground the common, lowly placed men and women more than those in power. Novels like *The Circle of Reason* (1985), *The Shadow Lines* (1988), *The Calcutta Chromosome* (1996), and *The Glass Palace* (2000) depict the conflicts related to intellectual, social and political disturbances that are rooted in colonial loss of power, and unjust dominance.

The formation of a 'self' is consciously attained by a community after its people after have undergone a prolonged struggle for political freedom. In his novel *The Glass Palace* Ghosh's characters experience the awakening of a spirit of resistance to the dominance of another race, culture and nation. While some experience a conscious awakening, many others only undergo the suffering brought about by the loss of the freedom and dignity. In critiquing colonial imperial governance of the British over India and other countries, Ghosh examines also its continued legacies in the twentieth century.

In this paper I propose to analyse the formation of the self among colonized countries that the novel *The Glass Palace* has portrayed. This novel depicts the history of India and Burma (Myanmar) from about 1885 to 1990s, referring to some of the most significant political and economic developments of this period, mainly in Burma. It however does not depict the 'grand narrative' of history as much as it depicts several streams of histories flowing during the period, and part of the larger historical developments, moving towards these events. The novel holds the readers' interest through the depiction of several characters' lives as they live through the period of the colonial subjugation, awakening of a spirit of resistance and the movements that led towards freedom. Through some of these characters Ghosh has traced the histories of different social, political and economic developments during the turbulent hundred years and a few decades in the subcontinent. The focus of the novel shifts between portraying the historical background as well as tracing the making of new identities during this period, as Ghosh explains in the 'Author's Note' that follows the novel (549).[1]

Amitav Ghosh presents the re/making of identities in the very processes of conflicts and experiences of these conflicting ideas upon the minds and hearts of these characters. The formation of 'self' takes place within experiential encounter with the quotidian world, with the 'others' around, and through displacements, disjunctions and forms of alienations. For some perceptive and sensitive persons, the questions lead to an ontological quest, while many others may stop at a short distance in the journey of discovering the self. Cartographical explorations of the borders, spatial, temporal and psychological, lead one on to encounter different locations, cultures and ideas. The relationship becomes an encounter with others, making enquiry of one's own roots, background and place in the present. Loss of acquired, given identities can become a means of discovering/constructing new identities; sometimes the search may lead to an acute sense of trauma and deep anguish. The novel goes over such journeys into the losing and making of identities by people entrapped within colonial dominance.

The common experience of British imperial dominance that was shared by the two countries, India and Burma, brought together people with different ethnicities and religious faiths. *The Glass Palace* depicts how in the late nineteenth century the large multitude of population living in these countries found themselves in the harsh and rigid control of a vast political machinery that thoroughly destabilized the older political and economic systems. It is in such a turbulent time that an eleven year old orphan boy, Rajkumar floats into the city of Mandalay. He moves away from his native place, Chittagong in Bengal, in search of better chances of survival. His mother dies on the raft during the journey. As he enters Mandalay, the capital of Burma, he witnesses important historical events: the British imperial army entering the city, its swift and decisive conquest of Burma, the deposition and exile of the King Thebaw, his Queen and family. The young boy first becomes involved in the process of surviving; then, he goes on to take full advantage of the new economic opportunities offered by the British rule in Burma. He works hard, learns fast, and manages to build a small, secure business of his own.

This is one of the aspects of Rajkumar's character, and one phase of his life. The processes of adjustment, quests and travels across borders that Rajkumar goes through hold the epic-like novel together. He is one of the most representative characters in the novel as his successes, projects and views reflect those of thousands of Indians, who had travelled to Burma during the late nineteenth and early twentieth century, in fact till the time there was a movement in Burma to force the Indians living in Burma, to leave. Rajkumar's quick intelligence, hard work and easy going temperament make him survive and succeed in all kinds of adverse situations.

Rajkumar and Dolly, the beautiful handmaid of the Queen Supayalat whom Rajkumar begins to love, as he saw her the night he went to the Burmese King's Palace, are both fairy tale orphans. Coming from an unknown background, they do not belong to any country and family. Yet they construct their 'selves' through their (un)conscious efforts at belonging and surviving. If Rajkumar migrates to Burma from India, Dolly has to follow the reverse route. She agrees to accompany the exiled King, his Queen and their three daughters when they have to live in India. Dolly's sense of duty and service to the Royal couple, even if they are leading the lives of powerless prisoners, reflects not a weakness, but a great inner strength.

Rajkumar and Dolly come together through Rajkumar's persistence, perseverance and will-power. Dolly has to be pushed into giving up her role of service and to think of her own life and happiness. After their marriage Rajkumar and Dolly have a happy life together, but after a few years, their personalities change, following the inherent, inner tendencies of their nature—Rajkumar remaining involved in worldly pursuits, enjoying physical pleasures and social status, while Dolly withdraws inwards, becoming more religious. Her involvement with the family holds her into the worldly activities, but she decides finally to enter a religious order. Her cultural and religious background now becomes dominant, and she leaves the family fold.

For Rajkumar and Dolly the rule of monarchy remains an unchallengeable order. Living in their given situation, they focus mainly on coping with the demands made on them. The larger political contexts of the empire are not understood by them, although the situations may raise some doubts and questions. As a child, Rajkumar wonders why the Indian soldiers fight for the army of their own conquerors (39, 40). He discusses the issue with John Saya, the elderly man who befriends him and later becomes his mentor. The anomaly of fighting for the power that is conquering other free people bewilders him. The question is answered much later, when the young Arjun and Kishan also ask the question.

The questioning of such political issues becomes more marked among the educated middle class characters in the novel. The Bengali middle class had during this period become more receptive to the western education introduced in India, and had also begun to question—both, the orthodox Hindu customs and social practices, as well as the imperial dominance. Characters who become aware of the unjust and unfair regime raise questions about the psychology of power as it plays between the ruler and the ruled. Queen Supayalat's resistance to the British rulers is an outcome of her own experience, though she too had weilded excessive and often unjustly, the power of a monarch. It is in characters like Beni Prasad Dey, Uma Dey, Arjun and Kishan Singh that the awareness of the injustice of the colonial regime brings a new insight into political and social miseries that the colonial subjects experience. They struggle within their existing mental attitudes which they had acquired from the prevailing social milieu; they gradually realize that their social world itself was deeply coloured by the ruler's discourse. The struggle between received notions and the ground reality about the nature of power which had such a control over their minds, psyche and entire culture, leads them towards a deconstruction of their colonial selves.

Beni Prasad Dey has a brilliant academic record, and after a rigorous preparation at Cambridge University, enters the prestigious ICS. He is, in his appointment as the Collector of Ratnagiri, virtually the goaler of the exiled Burmese King Thebaw, Queen Supayalat and their three daughters. The royal family is house imprisoned, without the freedom that even an ordinary person would demand as a right in a civil society. B.P. Dey's complete subservience to the British Governments' ideological discourse is exposed as he argues with the King and Queen, on different occasions, to defend the British Empire, its legal system and claims it being the most just and legal, civilized country in the world. His subservience to the Britisher's supremacy is well reflected in an exchange between him and King Thebaw, who was in the habit of getting into a political discussion with Dey. On one occasion, discussing the fate of Japan's war with Russia, the Collector goes a little too far in his praise of the strength of the British empire. He goes on to speak brusquely with King Thebaw: 'Britain's Empire is ... already more than a century old, and you may be certain, Your Highness, that its influence will persist for centuries more to come. The Empire is such as to be proof against all challenges and will remain so in the foreseeable future. I might take the liberty of pointing out to you, Your Highness, that you would not be here today if this had been pointed out to you twenty years before ... .' Such bold and brash words affront the dignity of the King, who 'flushed, staring speechless at the collector'. It is the Queen who responds with befitting sense of authority "She leant forward, digging her long, sharp fingernails into the arms of her chair. 'That is enough, Mr Collector', she said, 'Enough, *bas Karo*'" (107). The bureaucrat's excessive faith in the Colonial masters also reflects the sense of power he feels he shares with them.

B.P. Dey becomes a stooge in the hands of the rulers, as he keeps watch over the family. He has lost his human insight into the problems of a family with growing up children. After twenty years in Ratnagiri, the Burmese princesses have grown into young women, whose need for marriage are to be recognized. The British rulers try to play matchmaking, but have no idea about the actual cultural and social ideas that are to be looked into before proper matches could be found for them. In such a situation, the eldest daughter falls in love with the son of the coachman, who lives within the bounds of their house. When he learns of the alliance Dey cannot think beyond the scandal that the relationship would cause, both in public and at the government headquarters (149–50).

Beni Prasad's shocked and rigid responses to the human emotions and passions that govern the young men and women reflect his own inner dryness. His wife Uma comes from a Bengali middle class, a *bhadra mahila* whose entire physical and psychological being had been formed after a large scale social debate had gone on over the formation of modern Indian woman. Beni Prasad's behaviour with Uma is governed by a desire to mould her into a complete shadow of himself—so that she acts only at his guidance and will. He does not want to allow her the freedom to form her own relationships of friendships, of sharing secrets with Dolly about the lives of the princesses, or even Dolly herself.

The realization of the limits of his imagination and freedom strikes Beni Prasad after the two disclosures that the Queen makes about the First Princess; the shock is further aggravated by the disclosure that Uma had known about the situation but she had not shared the information with him. He is deeply pained at the lack of trust and confidence by Uma (153), although he does not still try to probe within himself why he could not win Uma's trust. He realizes that he has failed in many ways, but his internalization of the British colonial values, culture and ideology have gone a long way into inducting within him the British norm. Uma feels this when he questions her, 'she began to sob, covering her face with her hands. The wifely virtues she could offer him he had no use for: Cambridge had taught him to want more ...' (153). He chooses death by sailing out in a damaged boat, and escapes public humiliation. The sense of superiority he had felt as an official of the British Empire deserts him as he realizes his subordination to a vast impersonal and harsh system.

The struggle to become free of the acquired colonial mentality becomes a means of reconstructing the self for those who attain the awareness. Beni Prasad, Uma Dey, Arjun and Kishan Singh go through the various states of such awareness and destabilization. Arjun and Uma reflect the new political questioning of the colonial hegemony and social norms that began to be formed in some sections of India. Their personal awakening makes them more suspectible to sharing the larger consciousness, as each goes through his/her experiences.

Uma's marriage with the ICS officer is regarded by all her relatives to be her good fortune. But she finds the marriage to be an emotional strain as her husband tries to mould her into his own image, the colonial model of a perfect companion. Uma's status as the Collector's wife brings her into public stage and she has been prepared for playing the role in her upbringing as a *bhadramahila* which however has been shaped by the nationalist imagining. She has received the benefits of the new designing of apparel, conduct and relating to people outside the close circle of family members. That the preparation was in itself an important agenda for the social reformists and thinkers in India is brought out in the diaries, speeches and writings by men and women of that period. Recent research into social history of the period between 1880–1940 records the efforts that were made to create a 'new' feminine model to be suit the new social cultural milieu that was taking shape.[2]

Uma conducts herself with a demeanour that reflects her inner strength, alertness and sensitivity to the needs of others. She becomes friendly with Dolly, helps in arranging meeting between Rajkumar and Dolly, although her husband, Mr Dey, does not fully appreciate the idea. Her husband's wish to control her fully, mentally as well as physically, balks her as she realizes that it amounts to another form of slavery—a total submission to another person's will: 'The wifely virtues she could offer him he had no use for: Cambridge had taught him to want more; to make sure that nothing was held in abeyance, to bargain for a woman's soul with the coin of kindness and patience. The thought of this terrified her. This was a subjection beyond decency, beyond her imagining' (153). Uma's self respect refuses to submit to such a relationship and she decides to leave him, to walk out of the marriage.

The rebellion against extreme submission does not have only a personal cause. She also resents her husband's insensitivity towards the others who have been deprived of their rights, dignity and freedom, specially the king and his family. Uma's reaction was an extreme one, unusually bold for the times. Her social prestige as the Collector's wife was enough to tempt any woman into quiet compromise. But, like Mrinalini, in Tagore's short story *Streer Patra* (1914) she rejects her own social security and prestige to voice her resentment against unjust domination—by a person, and a system.

Uma's search for her dignity and own independent life continues till the end of her life, as she soon becomes involved with the Nationalist movement. Like a large number of women from the middle class and the elite strata of society, she too becomes involved in the political struggle and begins to devote all her energies to the cause of freedom. She travels to other countries, meets many new people, in the process becoming an individual with a self-awareness that was constructed through many struggles. Her education and inner boldness have helped her in her encounters with new situations and different people. By transcending her personal needs, she merges herself into the national cause and learns to work constructively for public good.

The last scene of her life in the novel, about her and Rajkumar, reflects an enigmatic relationship, again highlighting her ability to leave the past behind her and live in the present. Ghosh has depicted the formation of the self through the characters' dialectical relations with different experiences, the ability to move against the tide, if need be. Specific social and political contexts are given in detail so as to locate the character's developments in the matrix of history.

Historical development of ideas and movements have deep impact on the formation of one's ideas. Rajkumar was a child in 1885, and could only raise a question about the Indian soldiers' carrying out the orders of their British masters (28–30). As he grows older he too soaks in the imperial economic interests and plays in that field, exploiting the opportunities without any consideration for the poor in India or Burma. About three decades later, Uma can question the Empire's injustice towards the masses in Asia, including the royal rulers who are also brought down to the level of commoners. She also protests against patriarchal exploitation of the women. Arjun, her nephew, can go much further in questioning the immorality of the Empire when he becomes an officer in the British Imperial

Army during the 1940s. He explores the colonial propaganda of creating a modern United India, after his own disillusionment. Through these different characters Ghosh presents the changing awareness of the different generations of Colonized Asians.

Arjun's pride in being an Army officer reflects the prevailing social importance attached to holding a position in British bureaucracy and services. He can see critical responses to his position when he meets some of Uma's fellow nationalists at home or in the streets of Calcutta, during the marriage of Manju. He echoes the colonialists' claims that the Indians in the British Services are the first true Indians, for they have left behind the considerations of caste, religion and orthodox rituals in their food habits, etc. He and his friends in the Army claimed, 'Look at us—' they would say,—'Punjabis, Marathas, Bengalis, Sikhs, Hindus, Muslims. Where else in India would you come across a group such as ours—where region and religion don't matter—where we can all drink together and eat beef and pork and think nothing of it?' (278). It is not apparent to him that he has simply become a mimic man, whose own socio-cultural frames of values have been lost, and who now has really no identity of his own. In discussions with Dinu, one of Rajkumar's sons, he boasts of being more modern than any other person around him; of being really 'free' (279).

When fighting for the British rulers in the battle-fields of Burma, the implications of the full extent of his slavery become clear to Arjun. Several other army men—officers and those in lower ranks have begun to ask the question that had disturbed the young Rajkumar—why do the Indians fight the wars against other free people, on behalf of their colonial masters. Kishan Singh, his attendant, brings to him the historical awareness of the slave people, as he tells Arjun about the extreme terror created by the British after the failure of the war of independence in 1857 (429). Arjun's realization that he had been completely controlled by the milieu of subjugation in which he lived, and he had actually acted out the will of the colonial masters, becomes a searing self-knowledge for Arjun. He looses his confidence and pride as a young Indian, for he now sees a horrible image of himself—in his own eyes. To make this awareness more graphic at this point Ghosh uses the image of the moving of the potter's wheel as it shapes the formless clay into small vessels and other objects. Arjun has a hallucinating vision in which he finds himself and Kishan Singh among the millions of others who were shaped by the invisible hands of the masters of their fate—the rulers. 'He had a sudden hallucinatory vision. Both he and Kishan Singh were in it, but transfigured; they were both lumps of clay, whirling on potters' wheels'. Although he, i.e., Arjun, had felt the touch of the potter's hand he did not have any recollection of it anymore; it surprises him, how could he be 'no longer aware of the pressure of the potter's hand, unconscious even that it had come his way', while Kishan Singh, less educated than he 'should be more aware of the weight of the past than he, Arjun?' (431). This amnesia perhaps reflects the condition in which the middle class lived, thus able to imitate and obey the colonial masters more easily. He is shocked to realize that despite his faith in his own freedom of choice, there had never been any such freedom available.

Kishan Singh's discussions with Arjun in the battlefield lead Arjun towards a moral awakening: he decides to give up fighting for the imperial rulers and to become responsible for his fate. It leads to an awareness of truth—about the his own enslavement and his duty to his country and the oppressed people. He travels a vast distance in his search for the self that is not of a slave but of a free, self-defining person.

Resistance becomes an important strategy for gaining a self that has its roots in one's own history and experience. Recognizing the forms of enslavement and reacting against it also are governed, to some extent, by social, political awarenesses, but the self-generated activism plays an important role as well. Ghosh makes the self as an ever growing adaptive and fluid inner awareness, that may bring about its end, or survive through action. The novel *The Glass Palace* is a gallery of pictures that invite intense analysis and provides social insight.

Aung San Suu Kyi's public appearance in front of her house in the sixth year of her house arrest (1996) towards the end of the novel (last but one Chapter, 47) brings a dramatic end to the story that began a 101 years' ago with the entry of the British army into Burma in 1885. Dinu, Rajkumar's son, and Jaya, one of Rajkumar's grand children, witness this scene by the road-side, just as in 1885 the boy Rajkumar had stood near a road-side tea stall and heard the rumblings of the British guns. Aung San Suu Kyi (popularly known as Suu Kyi) is the daughter of Aung San, one of the leaders of Burmese national movement against British empire's rule. U Thant was tipped to be the first president of the free country but was assassinated before the event could take place. Years later, in 1990s Suu Kyi has become the leader of the Burmese people protesting against the imposition of military rule by Burmese. Suu Kyi has voiced the desire for democratic governance through totally non-violent methods.

As Dinu and Jaya watch the beautiful slim woman emerge in public, she stands quietly for sometime, then laughs in a peaceful manner, spreading the message (without using words) of hope and cheer. By not submitting totally to the power of politics Suu Kyi has, Dinu says, 'torn the masks from the general's face .... She has shown them the limits of what she is willing to do ... and these limits have imprisoned them too ... she haunts them unceasingly, every moment ... she has robbed them of words, of discourse' (542). She directs the movement through silence, absence and a well-maintained self-discipline. In her laughter and angerlessness she reverses the earlier struggles based on army strength, politics of power and the domination in which King Thebaw and Queen Supayalat were caught and lost to the superior British armed forces. Suu Kyi's defiance of the army's strength is attained through a civil obedience of the terms laid down by her jailers. By transcending her selfish personal goals and desires Suu Kyi becomes a maker of history rather than a victim of historical forces.

The struggle with adverse circumstances in which the different characters of this novel are caught becomes for them a testing ground. They test their inner resources and ability to face adversity and move forward to remaking the self. The awareness that comes in the wake of this process varies in the different person, in accordance with the distance they travel.

NOTES

1. Amitav Ghosh, *The Glass Palace,* 2000. Ravi Dayal Publishers, New Delhi. pp. 549–552. Ghosh refers to the 'near obsessive urge' that he experienced in the search he made through people, texts and documents for creating authentic locations for the various characters that he has created in this novel. It took him about five years, (Author's Note) to collect all this material.
2. Some of the essays that discuss these debates in detail are: Bharati Ray, 'The Freedom Movement and Feminine Consciousness in Bengal' from *The Seams of History: Essays on Indian Woman*. Ed. Bharati Ray. Oxford University Press 1995, pp. 174–218; Madhu Kishwar, 'The Daughters of Aryavarta' *Women in Colonized India: Essays on Survival, Work and the State*. Ed. J. Krishnamurthy. Oxford University Press 1989, pp. 78–85; Tanika Sarkar, 'Politics and Women in Bengal: The Conditions and Meaning of Participation'. *Women in Colonized India: Essays on Survival, Work and the State.* Ed. J. Krishnamurthy. Oxford University Press 1989, pp. 242–252.

REFERENCES

Ghosh, Amitav. *The Glass Palace,* 2000. New Delhi. Ravi Dayal Publi. Permanent Black. 2000.

Tagore Rabindranath. "Streer Patra". Original in Bengali, first published in 1914. 'Patni Ka Patra' translated by Ramsingh Tomar, in *Rabindranath Ki Kahaniya* Vol. I, New Delhi. Sahitya Akademi, 1961, 1962, pp. 357–372.

Contributors

U.R. Ananthamurthy is a leading contemporary Indian writer and critic. He is considered to be one of the most important representatives of the *Navya* movement. Ananthamurthy is the recipient of the Jnanpith Award (1994) and the Padma Bhushan (1996). His novels have been translated from Kannada into several Indian and European languages.

Preeti Bhatt is Assistant Professor of English, Malviya National Institute of Technology, Jaipur. She worked on Muriel Spark for her doctoral degree. She is now engaged in research on Indian Fiction in English, and is co-editor of *Contemporary British Fiction* (2007).

Bandana Chakrabarty teaches English at Government College, Kala Dera (Rajasthan). She worked on the short stories of Alice Munero for her doctoral degree, she co-edited (with Urmil Talwar) *Contemporary Indian Drama* (2005).

Esther David, trained as a sculptor, writes in English. She was Chairperson of Gujarat State Lalit Kala Academy and often teaches Art Appreciation at CETT University. She has published three novels, several short stories and also art criticism.

Mridula Garg, recipient of Vyas Samman for *Kathgulab*(Hindi) and the Hammet Hellman grant for courageous writing, has published six novels, more than eighty short stories and three collections of essays. She writes a regular column for *India Today*. Her work has been translated into several languages.

Santosh Gupta former Professor and Chairperson, Department of English, University of Rajasthan. She has co-edited (with P. Kar) *Rethinking Modernity* (2005) and (with P. Bhatt) *Contemporary British Fiction* (2007) and has written on Feminist and Postcolonial issues. She has recently completed a UGC Project on Modern Prison Narratives.

Jasbir Jain is former Professor and Chairperson, Department of English, University of Rajasthan. Founder Director of IRIS, she has published extensively on Postcolonial theory and issues. Among her recent publications are *Beyond Postcolonialism: Dreams and Realities of a Nation* (2007) and *Crossing Borders: Post 1980 Subcontinential Writing in English* (2009). Currently she is Sahitya Akademi Writer in Residence affiliated to the Department of English, University of Rajasthan.

Lakshmi Kannan is a bilingual writer writing both in English and Tamil. She uses the *nom de plume* 'Kaaveri', for her Tamil writing. Her recent work in English is *Unquiet Waters* (Sahitya Akademi). She is the author of several novels, collections of short stories, novels and poems. Her works have been extensively translated.

Nilofer Kaul teaches at Hans Raj College, Delhi. She worked for her Ph.D. on American and Canadian women writers. Nilofer is trained as a Psychoanalyst.

Uma Mahadevan is an IAS officer. She pursued her dectoral dissertation on Modern Fiction at IIT Mumbai. She reviews books for leading newspapers and has buplished papers on modern fiction and films.

Charu Mathur teaches English at the University of Rajasthan, Jaipur. She has worked for her doctoral dissertation on 'Perspectives on Women in the Selected Plays of Eugene O'neill and Tennessee Williams'. Her areas of interest are American and Indian drama, postcolonial literature and women's writing.

Mini Nanda is Associate Professor in English at the University of Rajasthan. Interested in British studies, she has moved onto Canadian and Canadian native traditions, Indian literatures and feminist studies. At present Nanda is working on Muslim women writers with special reference to partition novels and films.

Harish Narang is a reputed scholar and former Professor of English, Jawaharlal Nehru University, New Delhi. Narang has worked in African studies, translated several texts and written on the diaspora; his publications includes *Politics as Fiction: The Novels of Ngugi Wa Thiong'O* (Creative Books), and *Writing Black, Writing Dalit: Essays in Black African and Dalit Indian Writings* (Indian Institute of Advanced Studies, Shimla).

Uma Parmeswaran was Professor of English at the University of Winnipeg, President of Immigrant Women's Association of Manitoba, and member of the National Council of The Writers' Union of Canada. Her recent publications include award-winning *What was Always Hers* (short stories), *The Sweet Smell of Mother's Milk-Wet Bodice* (novella), *Mangoes on the Maple Tree* (novel). She lives in Winnipeg.

Sudha Rai, Professor and current Chairperson, Department of English, University of Rajasthan, Jaipur, worked for her doctoral work on The Expatriate Sensibility. She has a published a monograph on V.S. Naipaul and has written extensively on postcolonial writers including women poets. Rai has co-edited *Films and Feminism* with Jasbir Jain. She is the recipient of Senior Fellowship on Aboriginal Studies in Australia.

Rajee Seth has published nine short story collections and two novels. She also writes poetry, essays and literary criticism in India. She has been translated into many languages. Seth has translated one hundred letters of Rainer Maria Rilke into Hindi. Recipient of many prestigious awards, Rajee Seth has been a fellow at the Indian Institute of Advanced Study, Shimla.

Sudha Shastri is teaches English at IIT, Mumbai and has worked on intertextuality for her doctoral thesis. She has a wide range of interests and has done some work on dalit writing. Narratological studies are her major area of interest.

Nidhi Singh teaches English at the University of Rajasthan, Jaipur. For her doctoral dissertation she worked on 'The Mythic Reconstitution of Character and Place in the Novels of Rudolph Stow'. Currently she is exploring writers from Egyptian and Arabic backgrounds.

Urmil Talwar is currently a UGC Senior Research Fellow affiliated to the Department of English, University of Rajasthan. She is working on Border Poetics in the works of Amitav Ghosh. She has co-edited (with B. Chakravarty) *Contemporary Indian Drama* (2005) and (with S. Agrawal) *Gender, Culture and History: Inside the Haveli* (2008).

Index